Lucid Dreaming

An In-depth Guide Geared towards Novices: Unraveling the Methodologies and Scientific Principles Enabling Dream Control

(A Critical Handbook on Astral Projection and Extra-Corporeal Events)

Lukasz Russell

TABLE OF CONTENT

Understanding Lucid Dreaming 1

Methods for facilitating personal lucid dreaming experiences 7

Strategies to Elicit Lucid Dreaming 26

The Classification of Dreams into Five Categories 30

Sleep Well 59

What Actions Should Be Taken Upon Achieving Lucidity 82

Is Lucid Dreaming Dangerous? 100

Establishing an Ideal Haven 133

Techniques Of Lucid Dreaming 154

Develop Self-Awareness 181

Understanding Lucid Dreaming

What Is It?

In its most basic essence, lucid dreaming entails the ability to discern the state of being in a dream-like realm while in the midst of slumber. In this particular instance, one is capable of discerning their location, companionship, and dream actions with a striking clarity comparable to wakefulness. This may explain the findings of certain studies, which suggest that lucid dreaming shares similarities with the state of waking consciousness. Both states involve cognitive processes that engage the prefrontal cortex, a region of the brain associated with multifaceted behaviors such as strategic thinking, logical reasoning, memory formation, and personal growth.

Therefore, it can be concluded that lucid dreaming revolves around enhancing the clarity of one's consciousness, enabling one to discern the state of dreaming. It is imperative that you possess the capacity to identify the initiation of your aspirations, as it greatly influences your earnest involvement in pursuing said aspirations. As an illustration, in the event that you happen to encounter a dream involving one of the eminent scientists you greatly respect in reality, you may acquire a grasp on concepts that have proven challenging and obtain a more profound understanding of significant existential matters that have been somewhat perplexing to you.

Individuals who possess knowledge of lucid dreaming have the ability to achieve an elevated level of cognitive awareness within their dreams, enabling them to conjure desired fictional characters such as their object of affection, admired figures from the realm of music or cinema, paragons of virtue, and so forth.

While ongoing research endeavors to determine the most effective methods of initiating and inducing lucid dreams in individuals who do not typically experience them, there remains a dearth of substantiated evidence supporting the notion that inducing lucid dreaming is a straightforward task. Nevertheless, various studies have indicated the potential to enhance both the frequency and duration of lucid dreaming. What would be the rationale behind such a requirement?

Acquiring proficiency in the practice of lucid dreaming will be immensely beneficial in regards to managing and regulating one's thoughts, imaginative faculties, and mitigating the occurrence of recurring nightmares. When one attains mastery in the practice of lucid dreaming, an expansive realm of possibilities and boundless potential emerges, enabling individuals to fully explore and manifest their aspirations within the realm of their dreams. Certain individuals who possess the ability to control their dreams have taken it to the extent of summoning deceased individuals with whom they were once emotionally connected, in order to share cherished moments and seek resolutions to inquiries that have been left unresolved since their passing. Additionally, it has become increasingly common for therapists to incorporate lucid dreaming into their treatment protocols for individuals suffering from generalized anxiety disorders, depression, panic attacks, and various other psychological conditions associated with a patient's cognitive processes and mindset.

These therapists instruct individuals in the process of examining the limits of their aspirations by uncovering the concealed potentials inherent in the human mind, such as accessing precognitive and telepathic knowledge during lucid dreaming experiences.

Overall, it can be appropriately stated that lucid dreaming pertains to an individual's capacity to achieve a state of conscious awareness within their dreams, enabling them to actively manipulate their thoughts, characters, and the unfolding events within said dreams.

Throughout the course, you will be introduced to the prominent advantages of lucid dreaming, provided with guidance on cultivating and gaining mastery over this skill, as well as exposed to more advanced strategies and recommendations to develop your ability to discern dream states, enhance the occurrence of lucid dreams, and derive numerous additional advantages from this refined form of dreaming.

To commence, let us direct our attention towards examining several advantageous aspects of lucid dreaming.

Methods for facilitating personal lucid dreaming experiences

Okay, admit it. You exhibit a keen interest in the realm of lucid dreaming. Who wouldn't be intrigued? It is fascinating to contemplate the possibility of becoming aware of one's own dreaming state while still in the midst of it. Kindly refrain from feeling disheartened if you have yet to experience any lucid dreams thus far in your existence; today presents the optimal opportunity for its realization!

While it may be the case that lucid dreaming comes naturally to certain individuals while others may struggle to achieve it, Stephen LaBerge argues that lucid dreaming is indeed a skill that can be acquired through learning. However, similar to any acquired skill, one should not anticipate the ability to achieve lucid dreaming instantaneously. In the event of impatience, failure is inevitable. It is crucial to comprehend that the attainment of lucid dreams necessitates the execution of a sequence of actions and the application of certain methodologies.

This chapter entails a comprehensive exploration of 8 straightforward recommendations or methods that will enhance your capability to readily attain lucid dreams.

1. Discern the distinction between reality and dreams (distinguish between the two!).

Acquiring the awareness of one's state of consciousness, whether it is a dream or reality, serves as the initial milestone in cultivating the ability to experience lucid dreams. Certainly, this observation appears quite evident, particularly when one is conscious. It is uncommon for one to simply confuse their reality with their dream. The more challenging task lies in discerning that one is in a state of dreaming while actively dreaming.

Although it may seem unusual, engaging in basic reality checks during moments of doubtful cognitive states can assist in discerning whether one is indeed in a dream. Engaging in actions like lightly squeezing your cheeks or engaging in self-inquiry regarding the state of being in a dream can facilitate the achievement of this objective. By doing so, you are effectively communicating to your brain that the current experience is grounded in reality, while the alternative scenario remains confined to the realm of a mere dream. With increased frequency of practicing this, you will develop the capacity to train your mind in recognizing circumstances that are more prone to being perceived as dreams. Consistently engaging in reality checks while dreaming can eventually serve as a stimulus to signal your brain of the state of dreaming.

A commonly utilized method by individuals to ascertain their state of being in a dream is to observe a clock or a timepiece, then avert their gaze momentarily, and subsequently redirect their attention back to the timekeeping device. In actuality, the passage of time will scarcely vary - merely by a few seconds at most. Nevertheless, within the realm of dreams, when we engage in the act of observing our clock or timepiece, briefly diverting our gaze, and subsequently revisiting the time display, more often than not, the indicated hour will exhibit a substantial disparity, serving as a conspicuous indication that we are indeed immersed in a state of dreaming. This tool proves to be highly effective in enabling us to recognize the state of dreaming. Therefore, I highly recommend attempting this technique frequently during one's dreams in order to serve as a catalyst for inducing lucid dreaming.

2. Write a dream journal.

Numerous authorities posit that maintaining a dream journal is a paramount practice to pursue for those aspiring to attain lucid dreaming. This is the designated space for recording the contents of your dreams immediately upon awakening. The precise timing of waking up, whether it occurs during the night or in the subsequent morning, is inconsequential. It is crucial that you promptly record your dream to avoid its subsequent fading from your memory.

We have a tendency to readily dispel our dreams upon awakening, as the recollections thereof are confined solely to our transient memory. Consequently, upon wakefulness, that memory will promptly regress. However, this will not facilitate the attainment of lucid dreams, as you will be unable to discern the nature of your dreams due to complete absence of recollection.

Diverse manifestations can be observed in the composition of your dream journal. It can be as rudimentary as a journal and a writing instrument. You simply need to ensure its close proximity throughout the night, either on your nightstand or nestled beneath your pillow. The concept revolves around the notion that you should possess the ability to promptly record your dreams without engaging in any additional actions. Placing your notebook at a distance necessitates an initial search, increasing the likelihood of forgetting your dream as new information supersedes it in your short-term memory during the search.

If one wishes to avoid unnecessary consumption of paper for a dream journal, an alternative course of action would entail utilizing a voice-recording device. Recorders are available in various iterations such as tape recorders, digital recorders, cell phone recorders, pen recorders, and numerous other types. It would be more advantageous for you to leverage recording devices as opposed to handwritten notes, as speaking allows you to freely express your thoughts without concerns about grammar or spelling errors, or the limitations of your penmanship.

Therefore, as you transcribe or document your dream, you will readily discern the recurring elements that frequently manifest in your dreams. These elements encompass acquaintances, former acquaintances, desired or visited locations, and any other imagery observed within one's dreams.

Furthermore, you will additionally gain the ability to discern certain dream indicators, or the manifestations that signify the state of being in a dream. It is widely recognized that within the realm of dreams, there exists a propensity for numerous peculiar occurrences that defy the constraints of reality, encompassing phenomena such as instantaneous transcontinental travel or the ability to soar through the skies. By recording these dream signs, you will enhance your capacity to recall them during dreaming, thereby enabling you to recognize them as indicators of being in a dream whenever they manifest in your dream experiences.

3. Modify your sleep schedule in accordance with the optimal time for experiencing lucid dreams.

Prior to embarking on lucid dreaming, it is imperative to engage in a restful sleep. Well, that is obvious. Nevertheless, mere slumber will not facilitate any progress. It is imperative to exhibit mindfulness towards your sleeping patterns in order to determine the optimal time during which you are most likely to experience lucid dreams.

Studies conducted on lucid dreaming have revealed a substantial likelihood of experiencing lucidity during a nap taken several hours after awakening in the morning. These studies have demonstrated that this temporal interval is the prevailing period during which individuals are prone to experiencing lucid dreams.

Additionally, there exists a strong correlation between lucid dreaming and the phenomenon of rapid eye movement (REM) sleep. During the process of sleep, REM (Rapid Eye Movement) denotes the phase characterized by the swift movement of our eyes beneath the closed eyelids. REM sleep is characterized by heightened brain activity and typically precedes the waking state. Consequently, it is highly probable for lucid dreams to manifest as we approach the waking state.

4. Consider utilizing the MILD, WBTB, and WILD methods.

Stephen LaBerge has proposed a method for individuals desiring to partake in the phenomenon of lucid dreaming, which he has dubbed the mnemonic induction of lucid dreaming (MILD).

Fundamentally, MILD refers to the process by which individuals establish mental connections or associations between their desired actions and the potential circumstances that may arise upon their execution. (Hence, it is referred to as mnemonic induction.) For example, as you walk past your quarters, you desire to be able to recollect the need to tidy it. It involves the act of recalling a previous memory in response to a concurrent event.

Therefore, when you retire to bed, simply affirm to yourself, "During my slumber, I desire to retain full awareness that I am in a state of dreaming."

To achieve this, it is necessary to be in a state of near wakefulness, as it is during this time that lucid dreams are most prone to transpire. Consequently, it would be advisable to adjust your alarm to coincide with the period of rapid eye movement (REM) sleep, occurring approximately between the fourth and seventh hour of your slumber.

Upon awakening, endeavor to recollect each fragment of your dream with utmost clarity. Recollect every detail with the utmost precision and lucidity. Subsequently, resume your slumber whilst maintaining the awareness that all occurrences are merely products of your dream state. Instruct yourself as follows: "It is my intention to retain awareness of my dreaming state when I dream." Repetitively engage in this practice until it is deeply ingrained, subsequently proceeding to resume sleep.

An additional methodology that could be of assistance is referred to as the "wake back to bed technique" or WBTB. With regard to this methodology, it is necessary to rouse oneself during the fifth hour of one's slumber. After regaining consciousness, direct your thoughts exclusively towards attaining lucidity. Following that, proceed to execute the MILD technique.

The final method to be discussed is the WILD technique, also known as the wake initiated lucid dream technique. As the nomenclature suggests, employing this particular method involves inducing a state of lucid dreaming through a state of wakefulness.

To execute the WILD technique, it is necessary to maintain unwavering focus on the desired dream content immediately prior to initiating sleep. Engage in contemplation and strive to minimize any sources of disruption in your surroundings. As you maintain awareness of your thoughts, gently transition into a state of slumber. This implies that you enter a state of slumber while retaining your consciousness.

Consequently, this assists in developing awareness during the initiation of dreams.

5. Practice self-remembering.

In order to achieve the realization of being in a state of dreaming, one must possess the capacity to retain the awareness of being in a dreamlike state. This technique is referred to as self-remembering, which involves maintaining a continual awareness that one is in a state of dreaming.

Robert S. According to deRopp, who is a biochemist and esoteric psychologist, "self-remembering entails a deliberate detachment of consciousness from one's current actions, thoughts, and emotions."

In the framework of self-remembering, two distinct personalities are associated: the one who performs actions and the one who perceives and reflects upon those actions. Essentially, during the state of dreaming, you assume the role of the protagonist. You are the individual who portrays the scenarios within your dream.

However, in the context of experiencing lucid dreams, it is crucial to estrange oneself not only from the role of a mere participant but also assume the role of a detached observer. It is not sufficient to merely entertain one's dreams, as one must also exercise mindfulness and closely monitor one's actions. Your observer self must prod your actor self into recognition that you are merely immersed in a state of dreaming, consequently fostering consciousness and clarity.

6. Periodically evaluate your dream journal.

Upon commencing your dream journal, you have recorded the discernible elements within your dream. As the passage of time ensues and you progressively document additional entries in your dream journal, it will ultimately become evident to you the existence of recurring patterns within your dreams. Upon developing an awareness of these recurrent patterns, you will acquire the skill to discern the indicators that manifest within your dreams, particularly those that consistently recur.

As an illustration, should you observe a recurring presence of an individual whom you have ceased encountering in waking life within your dream, it would be prudent to regard this individual as a symbolic manifestation within the realm of dream signs. Continuously reinforce in your mind, and allow this reinforcement to permeate your subconscious, that the mere sight of that individual signifies that you are in a state of dreaming. After the concept has been fully grasped, it will gradually become apparent that one is merely experiencing a dream upon encountering that individual once more, or any other phenomenon that is perceived as a characteristic of dreaming.

Consequently, it is crucial that you engage in regular review of your dream journal to ensure constant recollection of the recurring dream indicators commonly experienced in your dreams.

7. Engage in periodic reality checks.

Conducting reality checks is crucial for attaining lucidity in one's dreams, despite potentially appearing inconsequential in waking life. As elucidated in the preceding section of this chapter, employing reality checks will assist you in discerning between experiences that pertain to the actual world and those that transpire within the realm of dreams.

Engaging in reality checks on a singular occasion will yield limited benefits. You must persist in this behavior until it becomes ingrained as a habitual practice. Once you have become accustomed to performing reality checks, you will instinctively engage in this practice whenever you encounter peculiar or atypical situations, particularly within the realm of your dreams.

Engaging in reality checks does not solely entail actions such as pinching one's skin or similar activities. Additionally, this entails undertaking various tasks, such as identifying the recurring symbols and indicators that have been documented in your personal dream log. Upon encountering a dream sign, one will eventually come to the realization that it is merely a manifestation of a dream, as one has ingrained the knowledge that said sign represents the state of dreaming.

Additionally, allow me to offer an intriguing suggestion to enable you to discern whether you are in a state of dreaming: should you happen to lean against a surface, it is typically the case that you will pass through said surface. Thus, upon experiencing the consequential outcome of passing through a solid surface upon exerting pressure against it, one should come to the realization that one's current state of consciousness is in fact a mere figment of one's imagination. That particular occurrence may also serve as a means of verifying reality.

8. Utilize symbols of clarity.

External factors can be significantly advantageous in facilitating the induction of lucid dreams. These aforementioned external factors are commonly referred to as symbols of lucidity.

Lucidity symbols encompass any objects or imagery that serve as reminders aimed at fostering an awareness within the dream state regarding one's current state of dreaming. Lucidity indicators need not necessarily pertain to one's desired dream content. It has the potential to encompass a wide range of possibilities, provided that its personal nature serves as a constant reminder of one's objective.

It is advisable to place your symbol of lucidity in a position where it will be readily visible to you upon awakening and opening your eyes. As an illustration, if you have selected a visual representation of stars as your symbol of mental clarity, it is advisable to affix the chosen picture to your bedroom ceiling or wall, enabling you to promptly encounter it upon awakening. Upon beholding the representation of lucidity, one shall be prompted to recollect their overarching aspiration, which is the attainment of conscious awareness within their dreaming state. As you gradually transition back into slumber, you shall retain consciousness, enabling you to perceive your dream state.

Strategies to Elicit Lucid Dreaming

Lucid dreaming presents a remarkable opportunity to delve into the depths of your subconscious and partake in extraordinary metacognitive adventures. In much the same way that individuals exhibit varying responses to various circumstances, multiple methodologies exist for facilitating the onset of a lucid dream.

Through diligent practice, you will acquire the skills to experience vivid lucid dreams that are indistinguishable from reality.

Take into account the subsequent approaches to induction, with no specific sequence. Although there are shared characteristics among them, each of them exhibits slight variations.

Kindly take into consideration that the matter at hand pertains solely to your own person. The validity of someone else's claim regarding the best technique is inconsequential. This is your personal experience, thus it is incumbent upon you to determine and pursue the course of action that is most suitable for your situation.

WAKE-INITIATED LUCID DREAMING (WILD)

A wake-initiated lucid dream (WILD) occurs when one transitions directly into a dream state from the state of wakefulness. This is frequently accomplished utilizing specialized music known as binaural beats or through the utilization of guided hypnosis.

Binaural beat therapy represents a nascent modality of sound wave therapy. It capitalizes on the premise that the auditory apparatus discerns a unified tone despite the slight differentiation in frequency experienced by each ear. The efficacy of inducing lucid dreams can be attributed to the impact of binaural beats on altering the frequency of brain waves. Given that lucid dreams generate heightened gamma brain activity, employing binaural beats operating within the gamma frequency range will most effectively facilitate the induction of lucid dreams.

One should aim to achieve a state of complete relaxation and utmost comfort in order to effectively accomplish this task. To achieve complete immersion, utilize headphones and an eye mask.

You select the music based on personal preferences. For newcomers, initiating with an act of attentive listening to a guided meditation can prove to be beneficial. Whilst engaged in attentive listening, one can develop the ability to maintain cognitive awareness while entering a state of sleep-induced physical relaxation.

Essentially, it is possible to acquire the ability to achieve absolute bodily relaxation to the point where it assumes the role of your physical representation. After the avatar has entered a state of slumber, your gathering may commence.

WILD possesses a straightforward nature, yet proves challenging to acquire proficiency in.

Engaging in alternative methods of inducing lucid dreams can enhance the likelihood of experiencing Wake-Induced Lucid Dreams (WILD).

The Classification of Dreams into Five Categories

The initial one among the five is recognized as indulging in reverie. In this cognitive state, one remains conscious, yet lacks full engagement with the surrounding events. Daydreaming is a prevalent phenomenon, and empirical evidence suggests that individuals engage in daydreaming for approximately 70 to 120 minutes each day during their waking hours. During a state of reverie, an individual enters a mesmerized mental state, wherein latent thoughts, memories, and ideas are brought forth into existence. Daydreams commence with a captivating notion or recollection, upon which your faculty of imagination assumes control. Certain studies have indicated that individuals who engage in daydreaming more frequently possess a heightened proclivity for achieving dream lucidity during sleep, in contrast to those individuals who do not partake in such immersive mental wanderings. This is primarily attributable to the fact that daydreaming entails the deliberate exercise of lucid dreaming. Daydreams are really great. They provide a wholesome means to temporarily transcend the mundane, alleviate frustration, or detach oneself from a harsh reality.

The second category pertains to a typical dream. The typical dream manifests itself during an individual's rapid eye movement (REM) phase of sleep. Typically, when you attain a duration of eight hours of sleep per night, approximately 100 minutes of that time will be devoted to the experience of dreaming. The dreams that are more vibrant and have a greater duration tend to manifest shortly prior to awakening. Dreams are remarkable due to the frequent instances where one remains unaware of the dreaming state until the awakening moment. Within the depths of your subconscious lies the mechanism by which you willingly embrace the reality presented in your dreams, perceiving it as truth in the fleeting instant it occurs.

Next is the lucid dream, the main focus of this book and they really are the best type of dream to have. During a lucid dream, one experiences an unparalleled sense of liberation and boundless potential. You possess authority over your dreams and have the capability to direct them towards any desired path. There exist two factors that delineate a lucid dream. The initial step involves being cognizant of the fact that one is immersed in a dream state, whereas the subsequent step pertains to the capacity to exercise dominion over the dream or guide one's focus. Lucid dreams offer profound insights into the depths of your unconscious mind.

The classification of dreams known as a false awakening pertains to the fourth type. This accurately reflects the intended meaning. Upon awakening, you proceed with your customary morning regimen, only to discover that you have not truly emerged from your slumber. It is conceivable that you might reach the point of entering your office building before becoming aware that you are actually dreaming, subsequently resulting in awakening. False awakenings manifest as highly vivid dream experiences. It appears that your cognitive processes are facilitating your upright movement from bed and enabling you to execute your usual activities. All the intricacies and nuances of the room are present. The alarm clock undergoes a time adjustment, while the sun gently emerges through the window coverings, imparting a palpable sense of body motion. Such dreams typically culminate in a surprising disclosure. One may observe themselves regressing to their teenage self while looking in the mirror, or during their commute to work, they may notice an absence of any other vehicles on the road. Ultimately, one rouses from slumber and comprehends that one had been immersed in a reverie.

Ultimately, the last and foremost formidable category of dreams consists of distressing and frightening experiences, commonly known as nightmares. Each and every one of us experiences them, and despite our best efforts to steer clear of them, there is a limited amount that can be accomplished. Nightmares ought to be infrequent events, typically brought about by factors such as stress, trauma, substance abuse, certain illnesses, and occasionally, the viewing of horror films can serve as a catalyst for a nightmare. The final point lacks scientific substantiation and remains merely a hypothetical notion. Nightmares typically exhibit a high degree of visual clarity, paralleling the experience of false awakening. Occasionally, they possess such vividness that they elicit a response from your sensory faculties, causing you to experience emotions or even specific forms of discomfort. Nightmares are indisputably the most disquieting among all dreams. Nevertheless, one has the capacity to convert a frightening dream into a lucid dream, wherein one gains the ability to manipulate the occurrences within the dream. One of the numerous advantages of lucid dreaming is the ability to assume command over a nightmare.

Go Bike Riding

Do I intend to imply that you should actively pursue all of those things? No. I would like to inform you that by adopting a state of unwavering openness, you will be granted the opportunity to engage with the suitor alongside all the aforementioned belongings. These identical attributes can be observed among individuals, regardless of their socioeconomic status, across nations. However, the pursuit of happiness involves more than just acquiring wealth. If such were the case, your happiness would perpetually elude you.

However, individuals within the specific financial bracket corresponding to the kind of enjoyment you seek are available, provided you are willing to liberate yourself from the confines of your subconscious constraints. On the following day, it is advised that you visit a nearby bicycle store and acquire a pristine bicycle. Discover the extensively traversed bicycle routes within your locality, frequented by individuals who align with your aspirations for personal development and professional growth. Commence cycling to that location for a minimum duration of twenty-one days, without harboring any expectations.

The remainder of the task will be executed by your subconscious mind. In due time, you will inevitably cultivate an entirely new cohort of acquaintances that will complement your existing social circle. Through the association with your new companions, an array of potential suitors shall emerge naturally and without strategic intervention, satisfying your inclination for romantic connection. What precipitated this occurrence for you at the present moment, rather than in previous times?

Previously, your ability to find a suitable partner was effortless, whether it be within your workplace, community, or in a familiar setting. However, should you desire to encounter individuals who deviate from the norm as a prerequisite, you will be compelled to venture into unconventional realms. Furthermore, you regained the freedom that you possessed during your childhood. Both sexes exhibit a greater affinity towards the liberating essence of one another, prioritizing it over physical appearance or financial status.

When the object of your affections observed you engaging in an activity that they deemed atypical for your character, an immediate attraction was sparked within them. The new challenge you will encounter is determining how to choose among the numerous prospective suitors. The subsequent observation you will make is that these prospective suitors possess superior qualities compared to the individuals who were previously attracted to you.

Bear in mind that it is you who underwent a transformation, not the suitors. Previously, you exhibited a rather dull demeanor, seemingly disconnected from the uninhibited essence of your inner child.

How can I ascertain whether this individual is suitable for me?

You will be able to ascertain, within a short span of time, whether or not this individual is suitable for you through the functioning of your amygdala. As previously mentioned within the context of this book, it has been explained that the amygdala, which is a specific region of the brain, serves the function of alerting individuals to potential threats or evaluating the suitability of others. In this scenario, it can be asserted that if one feels a certain level of attraction towards an individual, the amygdala will respond, akin to an intuitive sixth sense.

In this specific scenario, I kindly request that you refrain from experiencing any apprehension, and instead, exhibit determination to progress and establish a meaningful bond within the context of our relationship. You will consistently experience amygdala activation, not only in response to adversaries, but also in pursuit of advancement. When an individual desires to purchase a new automobile, the amygdala becomes activated. When the desire arises to purchase a new residence, embark on an entrepreneurial venture, or engage in conversation with one's ideal companion, the amygdala will initiate a cautionary signal.

The amygdala is merely triggering this alarm due to your lack of familiarity with this individual or your limited experience with advancing to higher levels. Numerous individuals, in the course of their lives, often retreat upon experiencing a sensation commonly referred to as a gut-feeling, which can be attributed to the functioning of the amygdala. The amygdala, which originates in the cranial region, manifests its effects much earlier than the sensation of discomfort in the abdominal area.

Therefore, in the event that you experience heightened caution signals and this individual does not exhibit an evident and immediate threat, it is recommended that you proceed with introducing yourself. You may recall that in your dreams, you would perform this action effortlessly. In your subconscious state, you would instinctively carry out this action without conscious deliberation, as the majority of inhibitions are rooted in the conscious mind.

The restrictions imposed by societal norms lack the capability to infiltrate and undermine the aspirations within the subconscious lucid state of mind, which is why one might engage in intimate experiences with unfamiliar individuals in the realm of dreams. Hence, one engages in intellectual debates or advocates for oneself, actions which are not typically exhibited within societal boundaries. I would like to emphasize the importance of fostering very high expectations for a new relationship as your next course of action.

Many major conflicts and arguments in relationships stem from having low anticipated expectations regarding cohabitation before actually living together. On this occasion, I implore you to refrain from withholding your true desires, which may result in subsequent remorse after a decade of married life. In this instance, fear signifies that you are indeed progressing towards personal development. Comfort indicates that you have reached the pinnacle of your developmental phase.

"When your green, your growing;
Once you cease, decay commences."

Ray Kroc

I kindly request that you enhance your perception of personal worthiness. By enhancing one's sense of entitlement, one can attain all desired outcomes in life, and receive cooperation and assistance from others. Allow me to provide an illustration of how your financial situation may be lacking equilibrium, indicating an imbalance in your life.

I presume that if I were to inquire about the remuneration you received for your initial employment during your childhood, it would likely pale in comparison to your current salary. If I were to inform you that it is advisable for you to resign from your present occupation and revert to your childhood occupation, receiving a remuneration equivalent to the amount you garnered during that period, what actions would you undertake?

Please be aware that I did not mention or suggest any kind of reduction in your expenses or giving up your car and current living arrangements. If indeed you were to engage in such an action at your present stage in life, it is likely that a prevailing opinion would suggest that you are exhibiting irrational behavior. Why? Due to the upward trajectory in both your professional growth and accrued responsibilities, it is vital to have a clear understanding of your perceived financial value.

However, what I have observed among the majority of individuals, both women and men alike, is a lack of efforts to enhance the value of their inner being.

As a result of the prevalent occurrence of spiritual harm in children from the ages of six to sixteen, it is unfortunate that they continue to receive inadequate support beyond this period. These individuals can be selected when a suitor who offers a salary of $3.65 per hour approaches them. I do not intend to imply that they earn that sum per hour, rather, I am suggesting that their behavior towards you is lacking in kindness and consideration.

If you should ever encounter genuine love in the forthcoming days, make certain that your potential partner possesses merits equal to the level of appraisal you expect from your employer when seeking a salary increase. Should you be seeking a life companion who possesses the capacity to assist in alleviating your emotional burdens, I implore you to maintain your current disposition.

In the subsequent page, a Journal Page awaits your perusal. This journal page is allocated for you to meticulously record the dream that you intend to solicit from your subconscious tonight, with the aim of obtaining elucidative responses upon awakening tomorrow morning.

The designated space on the page is intended for you to illustrate your lucid dream in a singular image, as it is widely acknowledged that a picture holds the equivalent value of a thousand words.

Inducing Lucid Dreams through Mnemonic Techniques

Mnemonic Induced Lucid Dreaming entails the practice of implanting cues within your subconscious that will serve as indicators of your lucid dreaming state. The technique involves iteratively reciting precise assertions that correspond to the dreams experienced during preceding nights. Continuously recite the directive until you attain a state of slumber. Thoroughly examining your dream encounters necessitates the maintenance of a comprehensive dream journal.

It is imperative to acknowledge recurring patterns that manifest in one's dreams. These phenomena are commonly referred to as dream signs. Given their frequent occurrence, contemplating upon that dream symbol in the event of its appearance would enhance the likelihood of attaining a state of lucidity, thereby increasing your chances of becoming consciously aware. As an illustration, individuals commonly experience dreams that pertain to aspects of their daily regimen. Numerous dreams are likely to occur in the environs of one's workplace, educational institution, or place of residence. Frequently, when we envision ourselves in such locations during our dreams, we readily assimilate the surroundings as if they were indistinguishable from our habitual professional settings in reality. This is seldom the situation. It is highly likely that the versions of our house, workplace, or school that we envision in our dreams will exhibit notable deviations. As an illustration, the arrangement could potentially be inverted, an additional set of stairs could be introduced where there was none before, and individuals who typically do not belong in those settings may be present. Upon pausing momentarily to examine our surroundings, it becomes evident that we are ensconced within a dream. If one frequently encounters school, work, or home scenarios within their dreams, it may be beneficial to employ this affirmation during the process of falling asleep.

In the event that I experience dreams pertaining to school, home, or work yet again, I will undertake a method of verifying my reality and come to the realization that I am indeed in a state of dreaming.

It is imperative to consistently engage in a process of verifying the authenticity of your experiences each time you physically enter any of these locations. This phenomenon will translate into a heightened ability to consistently execute the task within the realm of your dreams.

This method can also be employed for dream characters with whom you frequently come into contact. For instance, in the event that you frequently experience dreams featuring your canine companion, you may engage in the following affirmation ritual during the process of falling into slumber.

In the event that I were to have a dream featuring my canine companion tonight, I shall undertake a methodical assessment of my surroundings to discern the verity of the situation and consequently become aware of the fact that I am indeed within the realm of a dream.

For instance, it is imperative to consistently conduct a reality assessment whenever engaging with your canine companion to enhance the likelihood of successfully executing this task within a dream.

Meditation for Facilitating Lucid Dreaming through Mnemonics

Upon awakening and documenting a typical dream (one where lucidity was not achieved), we readily identify the instances within the dream where lucidity should have been attained. As an instance, a vision in which we engaged in dialogue with a deceased family member should have served as an indication of their absence from the realm of the living, and this interaction should be considered an irregularity. The occurrence of a dream wherein we consumed a peanut butter sandwich with great delight, despite being aware of our allergy in reality, ought to have served as a notable indication that we were, indeed, in a state of dreaming. This meditation follows the subsequent steps:

Envision yourself immersed once again in your most recent dream where you were unable to attain lucidity. From a first-person perspective, navigate to the specific segment of the dream wherein you desire to attain lucidity and proceed to conduct a reality verification. In the instance where I might engage in a dialogue with a deceased individual, I would inquire within my conscious self, "Am I experiencing a state of slumber?" Subsequently, I would make an attempt to exert pressure with my index finger onto the center of my palm, inspect any alterations presented in written text, and inspect the contents of my pocket to verify the presence of my envisioned object during the ethereal encounter.

Engage in this visualization meditation whenever you acknowledge the possibility that you could have attained lucidity. Meditate for 5-10 minutes.

Utilizing the 'Wake Back to Bed' Technique for Lucid Dreaming

This approach capitalizes on the heightened state of relaxation and deep concentration that one attains upon awakening. This approach exhibits one of the most impressive rates of success among individuals new to the practice of lucid dreaming.

Please adjust your alarm to rouse you 90 minutes subsequent to lying down or upon completion of a 6-hour period of sleep. After your alarm rouses you, promptly rise from bed and remain vigilant for a minimum of 10 minutes. Engage in the repetition of positive affirmations, thoroughly consume educational materials pertaining to lucid dreaming through reading or watching materials, and regularly practice reality checks. Then lie back down. After reclining, you may engage in mental imagery, envisioning yourself within the ethereal setting of your recent dream, and patiently anticipating its formation around you. Alternatively, you may choose to employ the Mnemonic Induced method while returning to a state of sleep. Additionally, one may engage in the Hypnagogic State technique detailed subsequently.

Sleep paralysis (the vibrational state) in relation to lucid dreaming

Should you possess the capacity to maintain cognitive awareness while your physical body enters a state of slumber, it is probable that you will encounter sleep paralysis. In this condition, your physiological response to voluntary attempts to initiate movement will be inhibited. Sleep paralysis occurs on a nightly basis to serve the purpose of inhibiting us from physically enacting our dreams. For numerous individuals, the encounter of sleep paralysis is reminiscent of waves of electric sensations, accompanied by buzzing and tingling sensations that are perceived throughout the entirety of the body. The initial encounter with this phenomenon can be both astonishing and disconcerting. Remain calm and composed in the event of encountering this situation. While it may cause mild discomfort, it does not fall under the classification of being painful. This presents an excellent chance to engage in the application of the Hypnagogic State Lucid Dreaming method.

Allow me to elucidate the process of acquiring the ability to induce and experience a sleep paralysis lucid dream:

Assume a position of rest and allow yourself to reach a state of relaxation close to slumber, while being mindful to refrain from completely succumbing to sleep. Maintain this state of relaxed trance. Maintaining a state of composed concentration on either the middle of the forehead or the perineum has been observed to result in the manifestation of sleep paralysis vibrations.

After experiencing the sleep paralysis vibrations, one can employ either the lucid dreaming technique known as the hypnagogic state, or endeavor to mentally depict the desired lucid dream scenario. When executed appropriately, it is probable that one will experience a state of altered consciousness known as a lucid dream. I would suggest that you delve into the realm of the vibrational state to uncover additional peculiar yet captivating phenomena. One can attain an extracorporeal encounter by inducing a particular mental state wherein one visualizes and simulates the act of rolling out of bed or ascending a rope. Conduct experiments and record observations to identify the approaches that prove effective for your particular circumstances.

"Hypnagogic State in the Context of Lucid Dreaming

This is an enjoyable activity. Please shut your eyes and observe and make a mental record of the visual sensations you encounter. As you attain a higher state of relaxation, you may gain the ability to discern subtle hues, outlines, and figures emerging from the depths of the darkness. Once you identify the specific colors, shapes, and images, endeavor to focus on them in a state of tranquility and observe the direction they guide you. Attempt to ascertain whether you can purposefully guide the hypnagogic imagery through the utilization of your imaginative faculties and deliberate volition. In the event that you attain a sufficient state of relaxation, it is plausible that you may eventually succumb to sleep, wherein these hypnagogic visuals have the potential to transform into a complete dreamscape. The crucial aspect is to maintain the state of trance. Apart from lucid dreaming, it has been found that this method exhibits efficacy when directing your gaze towards a wall. By maintaining a tranquil focus on a designated spot on an empty wall, captivating patterns and visuals typically manifest.

Presented herewith is an instructional exercise aimed at acquiring the aptitude to maintain a trance state.

Assume a supine position at a suitable moment when fatigue is typically experienced, and avail yourself of a brief period of restorative sleep. Please position your arms in a vertical manner, ensuring that your elbows are resting upon the mattress for support. In the event that you attain an excessive state of relaxation and succumb to drowsiness, your extremities will abruptly release their current restraints and startle you awake. The period encompassing the descent of your arms and the onset of slumber represents an optimal state conducive to the generation of hypnagogic imagery and the attainment of a lucid dream. Achieving a proficient ability to maintain a relaxed and elevated arm placement in close proximity to the state of near-sleep is paramount for acquiring the skill of utilizing hypnagogic imagery to induce lucid dreaming.

"Presented herein is an additional practice to successfully attain a state of sustained trance:

Completely fill a small glass with water until it reaches its maximum capacity, such that the surface tension becomes visibly convex. Please take a seat on the chair and securely grasp the glass of water. Achieve a state of deep relaxation, while ensuring that you do not succumb to slumber. In the event that you are excessively at ease, there is a likelihood of the glass slipping from your grip, thereby leading to the inadvertent spilling of water upon yourself. If you fail to achieve a sufficient level of immersion in the relaxed meditative state, the water's surface tension will remain intact, thereby preventing any droplets from falling onto your hands. The optimal scenario for this exercise entails a minuscule quantity of water gradually trickling out of the glass. This denotes a state of altered consciousness that is profound, yet not excessively profound to the extent of complete loss of awareness. This state is ideal for the experience of hypnagogic imagery.

Sleep Well

Could you kindly enlighten me on how your sleep was last night? Were you well-rested and rejuvenated in the morning?

Adequate, rejuvenating sleep is absolutely crucial for your well-being. It facilitates optimal functioning of both your physical and mental capabilities, and notably enhances your ability to experience vivid and conscious dreams.

On the other hand, extended periods of insufficient sleep result in chronic fatigue, impaired ability to focus, heightened irritability, and depression; additionally, it diminishes memory capacity and decreases responsiveness.

Suffering from sleepless nights and fatigued mornings has become a common occurrence in the modern, fast-paced society of today. In the past, individuals experienced enhanced sleep quality when residing in close proximity to natural surroundings.

Hence, establishing positive sleep patterns has become increasingly imperative.

The Most Effective Therapist Lies Within Your Own Mind

During my employment at a psychiatric clinic, I encountered a situation wherein I received a telephone call from a psychiatric ward concerning a woman in her middle age who had been admitted due to symptoms of psychosis, severe anxiety, heightened fear, and insomnia.

I encountered her during the identical afternoon. She arrived, took her seat, drifted into slumber, and remained asleep for a duration of one hour.

Subsequently, she awoken from her slumber and experienced a profound sense of well-being.

If I were of a younger age and possessed less experience, I would have roused her from slumber in order to engage in a conversation. However, thankfully, I possessed a more advanced age and comprehended the profound therapeutic capability that lies within the act of slumber. Therefore, I allowed her to take a moment of repose, and upon her departure, I conveyed the following sentiment: "This evening, I trust that you shall swiftly succumb to slumber and experience a restorative bout of deep sleep."

The following day, we reconvened and she expressed her utmost satisfaction with our initial encounter, despite my lack of action.

The crux of the narrative lies in my passive demeanor, where I simply abstained from any form of intervention. All she required was a secure refuge to relax, allowing the therapeutic power of sleep to alleviate her anxiety and apprehension. Sleep possesses immense healing potential, provided that one is able to attain a restful state.

This occurrence serves as a testament to the profound capacity of the human mind to facilitate healing. Furthermore, it is frequently observed that health care professionals achieve optimal outcomes by refraining from intervention and allowing the natural healing process to take place.

The state of dreaming possesses the capacity to facilitate the healing of psychological afflictions, while the state of profound sleep holds the potential to alleviate physical maladies.

Hence, physicians occasionally administer general anesthesia to stimulate innate healing mechanisms during a state of profound slumber for individuals with physical trauma.

10 Strategies for Achieving a Restful Night's Sleep

For optimal rest, it is advisable to maintain a dimly lit and tranquil ambiance in your bedroom, ensuring a moderate temperature neither too high nor too low. Maintain a minimalist aesthetic in your bedroom to minimize any potential distractions. Not too many books.

Ensure an ample duration of sleep and adhere to a consistent sleep pattern. Establish a consistent sleeping schedule by retiring and rising at identical hours on a daily basis. Please refrain from retiring to bed past 11 pm. Endeavor to enter a state of slumber during periods of darkness and rouse oneself upon the arrival of light. Obscurity triggers the secretion of Melatonin, the sleep-inducing hormone that regulates your sleep-wake patterns in a beneficial manner. It is advisable to avoid exposure to bright lights and screens prior to retiring for the night. Illumination diminishes the secretion of Melatonin.

Prior to retiring for the night, partake in a serene evening regimen. Rituals serve as cues to both your body and mind, indicating that it is time to initiate sleep. Engage in leisurely pursuits and detach from electronic devices. Gradually and gently awaken.

Maintain a nutritious and well-rounded dietary regimen. Avoid heavy, spicy food. According to Eastern traditions, it is recommended to abstain from the consumption of onion and garlic. Garlic has therapeutic applications but should not be consumed solely as a dietary supplement.

Engage in physical activity and expose yourself to the outdoors regularly, ensuring you receive ample fresh air and abundant natural light each day. Engaging in physical activity enhances the production of endogenous sleep-inducing hormones. It is advisable to refrain from engaging in physical activity in close proximity to bedtime, as it may disrupt your sleep.

Refrain from the consumption of alcoholic beverages, illicit substances, and tobacco products. Alcohol prevents REM sleep. Refrain from consuming coffee and black tea during the late hours of the evening.

Engage in meditation or partake in guided meditations. Meditation has the ability to alleviate mental agitation, facilitate rapid onset of sleep, and augment the experience of vivid dreams.

Release excessive mental preoccupations and enhance your bodily awareness. Ensure a thorough integration with your physical self in order to establish a profound connection with your energy.

Ensure the cultivation of a favorable mindset, particularly prior to retiring to bed. The ultimate contemplation, the final visual, and the ultimate sensation prior to slumber persist throughout the entirety of the night.

Conventional Tibetan practices involved individuals orienting their heads towards the East or North in their sleeping arrangements in accordance with the sun's movement and origination. You are encouraged to experiment with different approaches to determine which direction proves most effective for you.

Cultivate a constructive mental outlook.
It is crucial to cultivate a positive and tranquil state of mind prior to entering into slumber. The final thought that occupies your mind, the last visual impression that registers, and the ultimate sensation that permeates your being prior to falling into slumber retain their presence throughout the duration of the entire night. Hence, it is imperative to maintain a positive emotional state if one desires to avoid engaging in negative thoughts and behaviors throughout the entirety of an evening.

What evokes a sense of positivity and warmth within you? It may encompass circumstances from present times or from one's childhood. It may originate from real-life experiences or even stem from a dream. It may originate from either a film or a literary text.

Could you envision yourself as a marine mammal gracefully navigating the vastness of the ocean, like a dolphin?

How about envisioning the descent of a snowflake, the rhythmic movement of a wave in the vast expanse of the ocean, or the ethereal presence of a cloud suspended in the heavens?

Would you be interested in assuming the role of a minuscule fairy nestled within a flower, gracefully swaying with the breeze?

How about the experience of being seated upon your grandmother's lap during childhood?

Are you interested in visualizing the image of your childhood dog or cat comfortably resting on your abdomen?

Perhaps focusing on maintaining a steady and slow pattern of breathing within the abdominal region or finding solace in harnessing your inner energy yields optimal results.

Maybe you would rather engage in contemplation of emptiness or contemplate the essence of the mind.

Envision anything that brings you joy, serenity, tranquility, and a sense of calmness.

Lucid dreamers effectively conquer fears and phobias in a secure manner.
If you are gripped by acrophobia, what serves as the impediment preventing you, in a dream state, from audaciously

propelling yourself out of an aircraft? Not only are you fully ensured, but you also have the ability to impede time, exercise control over your descent, and gently hover down to the ground. After conducting this experiment with clarity of thought at an altitude of 10,000 feet, visionary individuals have proclaimed a notable improvement in their fear of heights in the realm of wakefulness. In my capacity as a clinical therapist, J. Timothy Green detailed in his article on lucid dreaming and Post Traumatic Stress Disorder, managing a direstoutcome imaginable in a positive manner makes new neural examples in your unconsciousbrain to help beat the dread for good.

Encounter your revered figures within your lucid dreams.

There exists a plethora of individuals who serve as exemplars and inspire me to adopt fresh perspectives and conduct myself in an altered manner. This distinguished group includes esteemed figures such as Tom Cruise, Richard Dawkins, Barack Obama, Derren Brown, David Mitchell, David Attenborough, and Richard Branson. Furthermore, it is imperative not to disregard the individuals who have made their contributions in more recent times, notably Nikola Tesla, William Blake, Salvador Dali, and Michael Chrichton. There are no limitations or constraints in this context. Whom would you opt to encounter in your state of consciousness characterized by a heightened level of self-awareness and control, commonly referred to as a lucid dream? What inquiries might you pose to them? The potential consequences are invaluable, and the impact these exceptional lucid discussions have had on my conscious existence is substantial.

Lucid dreamers construct their narratives beforehand.

There exists an abundant scope for proactively manifesting any imaginable ideal scenario. By employing a combination of dream-induced and wake-induced methods, individuals proficient in lucid dreaming can meticulously orchestrate intricate dream narratives prior to sleep. The higher your level of enthusiasm towards the fantasy, the more likely it is to manifest. This, in and of itself, has the potential to produce lucid dreams through the creation of intentionally constructed scenarios designed to serve as triggers for enhancing perception and clear awareness during dreaming. In the future, when the desire arises within you to experience the sensations of sailing across the Mediterranean on a luxury yacht, snowboarding on Mammoth Mountain, or paragliding above the Grand Canyon, you will have the opportunity to do so.

Lucid dreamers appreciate the intriguing sense of liberation associated with the act of soaring through the air.

During moments of lucid dreaming, I engage in aerial locomotion, effortlessly soaring, levitating, or gracefully gliding to any destination I desire. It is thoroughly enjoyable, and when presented with an option, why would one opt for walking?

When one engages in air travel, their attentiveness becomes focused on the entirety of the experience. It suggests that it is indeed taking place. Despite acknowledging the possibility of falling, you maintain a steadfast belief in your ability to soar, audibly proclaiming "I am soaring," which ensures your triumphant navigation through the skies. This present situation confers a notable benefit. In my perspective, the act of lucid flying holds the utmost appeal and proficiency within the realm of my imaginative reveries.

Lucid dreamers perceive a distinct significance in their existence.

Throughout the past few years, I have utilized my Lucid dreams to merge my conscious thoughts - in order to comprehend the essence of existence. One dream suggested that the meaning of existence lay in discovering purpose in one's life. There appears to be no discernible rationale other than the possibility of me creating one. Upon conducting a more thorough investigation, it is discernible that this notion holds significant promise as it suggests that the value of life will increase in tandem with my consciousness. My current motivation may bear no resemblance to my motivation in the next decade or two. Therefore, my forthcoming objective within the realm of Lucid dreaming is to explore the underlying rationale for pursuing this particular occurrence. Insightful stuff.

The role of Lucid Dreams as a fount of inspiration

Every individual grapples with the pursuit of inspiration. It presents itself as being nuanced, specifically targeting individuals who possess a penchant for innovation, such as artists, marketing executives, or authors; thereby providing an exceptional means to find inspiration. Lucid dreams offer insight into the depths of your profound levels of cognition. The experiences and memories that escape your conscious awareness are effectively stored in your subconscious mind, awaiting discovery by whoever reaches them first during a lucid dream.

Better Sleep

One of the medical benefits derived from experiencing lucid dreams is the potential for enhanced, intensified, and increasingly restorative slumber as a result. It is remarkable, particularly for individuals with suboptimal sleep patterns, that acquiring a select set of essential skills can significantly enhance the quality of their sleep.

Engaging in the practice of lucid dreaming enhances one's level of consciousness.

This fundamental principle of clarity encompasses the concept of becoming increasingly cognizant. Becoming cognizant of the manner in which you are dreaming indicates that you are expanding awareness into the realm of dreaming. This state of mindfulness entails an elevated sensitivity to the essence of one's own consciousness (considering that a dream is composed of what other elements?). By gradually cultivating an awareness of your mind during the state of dreaming, you are simultaneously developing a heightened consciousness of its contents during wakefulness. It constitutes a manifestation of mindfulness, albeit in two discernibly disparate states of consciousness. Furthermore, what does not demonstrate improvement when one's awareness is heightened?

Instead of consistently engaging in impulsive actions driven by your thoughts and emotions throughout the day, which demonstrates a lack of awareness towards them (you are immersed in your contemplations and emotions, similar to being immersed in a dream without lucidity), you start to "awaken" and engage with the content of your mind. Taking into account your contemplations and emotions rather than being guided solely by them is an exceedingly commendable decision. It can effectively safeguard you from a multitude of challenges and bestow substantial tranquility.

Uncover the potential of making decisions

When one is engaged in the state of lucid dreaming, one becomes aware of the ability to exercise volition. One can observe the fantasy as it unfolds and opt not to alter any aspects, a phenomenon commonly referred to as a witnessing dream. In such dreams, one assumes the role of a passive spectator, akin to watching a film, without actively engaging and becoming immersed in its content, thus preserving its lucidity. Alternatively, one could opt to alter certain elements of the fiction, such as improving the conclusion. In any case, you are practicing the intensity of the decision. Subsequently, you proceed to exert mastery over that control and implement it into your daily existence. Are you becoming agitated with your superior? That is your decision. You possess the capacity to alter your viewpoint, to adapt your sense of identification, to awaken and take accountability for your own life.

Re-encountering a beloved individual who was previously lost

If you have experienced the unfortunate loss of a companion or relative in the past, one notable advantage of Lucid dreaming resides in the potential to reunite with those individuals. You have the ability to assemble them within the realm of your imagination, and establish communication with them as if their presence were unquestionably real.

You will awaken with fond memories of that individual, as if you had only recently spent time together. It is an exceptional means to part ways with someone in the event that you never had the chance.

In summary, as one continues to explore the possibilities of lucid dreaming, a multitude of applications inevitably emerge. Attempt to rely primarily on your own judgment and choices, and observe the outcome that unfolds. Each and every Lucid dream is maximized to its full potential. The realm of dreams and your conscious perception of yourself are intertwined, enabling you to leverage this realm as a valuable tool for deepened self-awareness and enlightenment. I deeply appreciate the abundant possibilities afforded by clarity; it grants me the ability to soar like a avian creature without fear of descending or navigate through formidable obstacles. I have the capability to visit anyone and undertake any necessary tasks.

Moreover, beyond the peculiarity of wish fulfillment, it provides me with a direct conduit to both the consciousness underlying the dream and my unconscious self, enabling me to overcome prior fears and anxieties and perceive myself in an entirely new perspective. It's amazing stuff. Similar to any endeavor that holds value, acquiring the skill of Lucid dreaming proves to be a task of complexity. Regardless, through extensive training and unwavering perseverance, anyone has the capacity to accomplish it. If you are unfamiliar with this concept, simply by reading this article, you have initiated the cultivation of clarity.

What Actions Should Be Taken Upon Achieving Lucidity

Now that you are airborne, it is imperative to consider potential destinations, individuals to meet, and other such engagements. It is imperative that one consistently engages their thoughts during the entirety of the dream, as an absence of mental stimulation greatly heightens the likelihood of waking prematurely.

While engaged in my airborne activities, I often ponder the prospect of visiting the Pyramids situated in Egypt. I consistently arrive at the destination within a few seconds, whereupon I instruct myself to soar through the air and descend gracefully into the waters of the River Nile. I submerge myself beneath the water's surface and proceed to part my lips, inhaling the surrounding air. Subsequently, I indulge in the exhilarating activity of swimming at astounding velocities that surpass human capability, all the while effortlessly breathing beneath the water's surface. This remarkable encounter is not to be missed, particularly when one has exhausted all possibilities of aerial exploration.

Upon awakening, whether immediately after rousing from a brief slumber or at your customary hour of arising, it is advisable to once more record your encounter. On each subsequent night when endeavoring to experience lucid dreaming, it would be advisable to peruse the details of your preceding lucid dream in order to revive your recollection of it.

"Methods for Inducing Lucid Dreaming

The phenomenon of lucid dreaming is characterized by a profound and varied encounter, which diverges in its nature for each individual. Suppose you desire to experience a lucid dream this evening; it is imperative to make the necessary preparations for your physical well-being, mental clarity, and optimal sleep environment in advance. Subsequently, establish your alarm to sound after a span of 6 hours. Upon the activation of the alarm, rouse from slumber and subsequently endeavor to return to sleep with the deliberate objective of achieving a state of lucid dreaming. During this transition, ensure that your muscles remain motionless as you gradually transcend into a realm characterized by vivid and captivating dreams. That can be considered the fundamental knowledge, at the very least. Now let us delve deeper into the subject by analyzing it in more detail.

Methods for inducing lucid dreaming tonight:

• Dedicate the remaining hours of the day to contemplating the concept of lucid dreaming.

• Consistently perform a series of reality checks utilizing proper methodology.

• Cease the use of electronic devices one hour prior to going to bed.

- Please adjust your alarm to sound in 6 hours' time.
- Begin your day by maintaining your eyelids gently shut.
- Return to a state of slumber with the deliberate aim of engaging in lucid dreaming.

At this juncture, it is imperative to note that the technique demonstrated herein entails slightly earlier awakening than your customary routine, but only for a brief duration. This exercise aims to stimulate and alert your cognitive faculties.

Rest assured, there is no need for you to disembark from your bed. The method, known as the Wake Back To Bed Technique, is designed for individuals with technical expertise. As the nomenclature implies, it encompasses the process of setting an alarm, stimulating the mind upon awakening, and subsequently returning to rest.

There exist strong justifications for this phenomenon; the brain exhibits heightened activity during the rapid eye movement (REM) sleep stage, which occurs in the hours preceding the natural awakening. If time permits, it would be advisable to visit the shop and procure essential sleep aids such as incense, pillow spray, and ambient noise. If you are lacking in time, endeavor to acquire fundamental meditation strategies for the purpose of achieving lucid dreams.

Firstly, allocate the remaining portion of the day to engage in extensive research on the subject matter of lucid dreaming.

This is the ideal starting point. Throughout the remainder of the day until your bedtime, devote your thoughts to the concept of lucid dreaming. Familiarize yourself with the subject matter through reading, engage in discussions with acquaintances, and ponder upon the actions you intend to undertake within your state of lucid dreaming. The essential factor lies in directing your attention towards the task at hand. You have chosen to peruse information on lucid dreaming with the intention of cultivating your subconscious faculties in the realm of lucidity. For a considerable number of individuals, the mere contemplation of attaining lucidity will suffice to induce lucidity. That is a clear and uncomplicated technique that you can employ henceforth.

Prior to retiring for the night, it would be advisable to contemplate the concept of lucid dreaming. Furthermore, imagine yourself attaining a state of lucidity during the course of your dream. Make an attempt at experiencing it firsthand, and henceforth, envision yourself achieving a state of lucidity multiple times throughout the day. It is expected to enhance the probability.

Proceed to the second step: Engage in a significant number of reality checks.

A reality check is employed to discern one's state of consciousness, determining whether they are in a state of wakefulness or sleep. It is recommended that you engage in reality checks approximately ten times per day. However, if your intention is to practice this technique tonight, it is advisable to conduct a minimum of 25 reality checks throughout the day prior to retiring for the night. "Allow me to present a step-by-step process for conducting a reality check to induce lucid dreaming:

Kindly extend your hand and, using your remaining digit, attempt to push a finger through the surface of your palm.
- Anticipate its success, and only upon its failure, acknowledge to yourself, "Ah, I must be alert."
- While anticipating its occurrence, inquire within yourself, 'Could this be a figment of my imagination?'

In a dream, the phalanx/es shall invariably penetrate the distal appendage, whereas such an occurrence remains implausible within the realms of reality.

- Perform this test repeatedly throughout the day, and eventually, it will manifest in your dreams.

When this phenomenon occurs within the realm of your dreams, the finger will pass through the surface of your palm, thereby indicating the state of lucidity.

This serves as a singular instance of a reality check. There are numerous variations available, yet research has determined that the finger palm push test is the most efficacious method, proven to expedite the ability to experience lucid dreaming. In due course, you may choose to explore additional reality verification methods. It is of utmost importance to bear in mind that should you endeavor to experience a lucid dream this evening, you must undertake these reality checks. Attempting to engage in lucid dreaming during nighttime hours is not beneficial; the practice should be initiated during the daytime. And that is the most optimal piece of guidance for a multitude of individuals, which is to conduct a greater number of reality assessments throughout the course of one's day. However, that constitutes merely a fraction of the issue at hand. Lucid dreaming is a highly intricate ability that cannot be acquired within a single night, nor is it within the immediate grasp of many individuals. While there is a possibility, it is probable that the timeframe for completion will be slightly extended. However, this outcome is acceptable as the ultimate rewards upon achieving the goal are highly significant.

Step 3: Power down all electronic displays one hour prior to bedtime

Immediately prior to retiring for the night, refrain from viewing any electronic displays. Please switch your mobile device to silent mode, ensuring that the alarm remains functional, and refrain from further television viewing. This occurs due to the desire of your body to generate sufficient levels of sleep-inducing hormones, which are impeded by the presence of artificial light. This, in my opinion, constitutes the most noteworthy technique for enhancing sleep quality. If feasible, dim or switch off the lights and engage in a brief period of relaxation; alternatively, devote an hour or so to reading a book prior to retiring for the night. This greatly contributes to your sense of calm and mental relaxation. One might also consider donning a sleep mask and engaging in the practice of meditation.

What is the significance of this matter?

Our physical forms possess a remarkable capacity for precision and efficiency. They were purposefully designed to initiate sleep upon sunset and rise in the morning, rejuvenated and brimming with vitality, coinciding with the sun's ascent. So why don't we? The reason behind this phenomenon lies in the artificial stimulation of our brains through the exposure to light emitted by various devices such as phone screens, LED light bulbs, and television screens, among others.

Consequently, this results in the stimulation of serotonin production within your body during periods when it is ideal for you to be unwinding and preparing for rest during the nighttime. Additionally, it inhibits the production of serotonin in your body, leading to challenges in initiating sleep and experiencing restful, profound sleep. The worst part? In the absence of monitoring your sleep patterns and engaging in exploratory measures, it may be difficult to ascertain whether your sleep quality is suboptimal or not.

One might not be aware of the inadequate amount of deep or REM sleep obtained during the night, leading to a state of perplexity upon waking up in the morning, pondering over the reason for their overwhelming fatigue. Numerous individuals arise after a duration of eight hours or longer of slumber, perplexed as to why they continue to experience fatigue and despondency. The reason behind this is the inadequate acquisition of profound or rapid eye movement (REM) sleep due to insufficient production of melatonin in your body during the previous night. It matters.

Step 4: Establish a recurring reminder at approximately 6-hour intervals.

Please ensure to set your alarm approximately 2 hours prior to your usual wake-up time. If your typical waking time is 9 o'clock, adjust the alarm to 7 o'clock. Select an alarm system that is capable of rousing you from slumber without excessive auditory intensity. You desire a source of tranquil and effortlessly audible content, while also requiring your mobile device to be positioned in close proximity for convenient turn-off access, all without the need to physically rise or open your eyes.

Select a melodious piece of music or a tranquil tone. Regardless of the alarm option you choose, ensure it does not possess a snooze function. Ideally, you want it to rouse you promptly once, and subsequently cease its activation. Upon setting your alarm, ensure that you have your dream diary readily available, accompanied by a functional pen placed atop it. Ensure that all of these items are easily accessible from the bed, thereby alleviating the need to exit the bed. Given that this approach is fundamentally based on the Wake-Back-to-Bed (WBTB) technique, it can be regarded as a relatively straightforward means of achieving lucid dreaming. Typically, one would observe that this approach tends to yield favorable outcomes.

Procedure 5: Awaken while keeping your eyes shut

This will prove to be the challenging aspect. You desire to awaken through the use of an alarm while maintaining closed eyelids. Maintain a state of alertness and vigilance, metaphorically speaking. This indicates the need to rouse your consciousness while maintaining your eyes closed. It is of negligible consequence if you briefly open your eyes, yet it is advisable to refrain from doing so. You have the desire to promptly return to slumber upon deactivating the alarm. This is the rationale behind the term "wake back to bed," as it entails momentarily awakening before returning to slumber. However, it is imperative to bear in mind a significantly important aspect. The subsequent phase, which is pivotal in achieving a lucid dream this evening, constitutes the ultimate stage. It involves the execution of a wake induced lucid dream, if you will. It bears resemblance to a fusion of the Wake-Back-to-Bed technique and a Wake Induced Lucid Dream. Due to the fact that you have arisen early, it is to be expected that your cognitive faculties will be stimulated, however, you will eventually resume sleeping.

Hence, we requested that you diligently carry out numerous reality checks to increase the likelihood of spontaneously performing them within a dream, thus attaining lucidity even if you inadvertently slip into a state of unconsciousness. It serves as a reliable contingency measure.

As the focus of our discussion revolves around techniques for achieving lucid dreaming tonight, I am presenting you with all the relevant information simultaneously. Reality checks can be employed in isolation as a technique; however, for optimal results in achieving lucid dreaming tonight, it is advisable to engage in a comprehensive approach. Therefore, the crux of this approach lies in the subsequent events that unfold. You have awakened ahead of schedule, deactivated your alarm, and currently remain in a state of wakefulness with your eyes shut.

Subsequently, you will maintain mental alertness while allowing your physical body to gradually enter a state of slumber. Presently, this may evoke feelings of unease if you have not previously engaged in this practice, as it may lead to the occurrence of sleep paralysis, a state whereby the physical form is immobilized while the consciousness remains alert and self-cognizant.

You will experience the sensation of your body undergoing a gradual shutdown, while maintaining a state of awareness within your mind.

Please do not fret; there is nothing to be fearful of.

It poses no potential threat or risk whatsoever.

- This is the method through which you can attain the ability to engage in lucid dreaming tonight.

Once you have engaged in this task repeatedly, it will become an enjoyable and straightforward endeavor.

- Despite the potential uneasiness and fear you may experience, it would be advisable to maintain a state of relaxation and refrain from attempting any movement.

As previously mentioned, you will assume a supine position, remaining conscious while your physical faculties remain immobilized. This phenomenon occurs because of the interruption experienced during REM sleep, which prompts the body to enter a heightened state of activity in order to swiftly return to the deep sleep stage. The crucial aspect here is to remain vigilant during this occurrence.

You will maintain mental acuity and cognitive engagement while your body enters a state of rest, thereby facilitating the immediate induction of a lucid dream. This phenomenon arises from the uninterrupted wakefulness of your mind throughout the process. I understand that sleep paralysis may evoke fear, however, I assure you that it is a common occurrence, devoid of any harm, and an integral component of experiencing lucid dreams. One should embrace this occurrence as it signifies progress towards achieving lucid dreaming, and signifies proximity to entering a state of lucidity within a dream.

Presumably, you have comprehended the information thus far and the experience of sleep paralysis did not cause undue distress.

Is Lucid Dreaming Dangerous?

This is an inherent inquiry, particularly for individuals experiencing lucid dreaming for the first time. Regrettably, the answer in question is negative. Lucid dreaming is widely regarded as being generally safe. While lucid dreaming generally poses minimal risks and is considered safe, it is crucial to acknowledge and address potential concerns and hazards. Therefore, I strongly recommend exercising caution while engaging in this practice. Are the perceived risks associated with this phenomenon overemphasized? A multitude of erroneous beliefs and misunderstandings persist regarding lucid dreaming, yet scholars have conducted considerable research on this phenomenon. In order to ensure a secure and pleasant lucid dreaming experience, it is imperative that you approach the realm of dreams equipped with ample knowledge and the appropriate level of preparation.

Presented herein are several widely recognized concerns, potential hazards, and misconceptions linked with the practice of lucid dreaming:

Experiencing sleep paralysis

The prevailing negative occurrence encountered by individuals who engage in lucid dreaming is sleep paralysis, which refers to the incapacity to exhibit voluntary movements during the state of sleep. Sleep paralysis is a prevalent and intrinsic phenomenon. It takes place on a nightly basis to prevent us from enacting our dreams. Sleep paralysis occurs when an individual transitions into the state of Rapid Eye Movement (REM) sleep. Given that we experience vivid dreams during the rapid eye movement (REM) phase of sleep, our bodily functions enter a state of paralysis in order to obstruct any attempts to imitate the actions taking place within the dream.

The realm of lucid dreaming exists within the transitional space between states of consciousness and unconsciousness, and transitioning completely into one or the other is easily achievable. Upon entering the stage of REM sleep and experiencing a lucid dream, it becomes feasible to attain consciousness while in a state of sleep paralysis. Nonetheless, the occurrence of hallucinations and foreboding sensations can concur during this phase of slumber, which, in conjunction with the immobilization, can invoke a sense of terror when encountered.

While it may evoke feelings of apprehension, acknowledging the potential and understanding its inherent validity can assist in surmounting any trepidation that may arise in the event that it materializes. The presence of fear serves to perpetuate and further exacerbate sleep paralysis, thereby sustaining its intensity and duration. The sole means of conquering paralysis is by embracing it and recognizing its inherent naturalness. This poses no threat and poses no risk to your well-being.

The phenomenon of sleep paralysis is not directly caused by lucid dreaming but is primarily influenced by one's sleep and lifestyle patterns. This condition may manifest in individuals experiencing sleep deprivation, heightened stress levels, anxiety, and other related factors. Notwithstanding, there is a possibility that certain techniques employed in the practice of lucid dreaming could induce episodes of sleep paralysis. I will provide a concise overview of these procedures as we will delve into a more comprehensive examination of various techniques in a subsequent chapter.

Dream Initiated Lucid Dreams (DILD) should be conducted without the involvement of sleep paralysis.

Wake Initiated Lucid Dreams (WILD): This method often involves the occurrence of sleep paralysis. Nevertheless, it can be regarded as an exceedingly efficacious approach to attain a state of lucidity, wherein one's awareness remains conscious despite the gradual descent into sleep of the physical body.

The MILD (Mnemonic Induction of Lucid Dreams) technique typically does not entail experiencing sleep paralysis, unless implemented improperly.

FILD (Finger Induced Lucid Dreams): It is plausible that this technique may lead to the occurrence of sleep paralysis.

Does the concept of lucid nightmares exist?

It is feasible to experience a vividly unsettling dream. Fortunately, it is a rarity to experience lucid nightmares. The vast majority of individuals who experience lucid dreams do not encounter any instances of fear or distress whatsoever. Similar to any other dream, lucid dreams have the potential to manifest as distressing or frightening experiences. Those engaged in the practice of lucid dreaming possess awareness during such experiences, consequently amplifying the sheer terror associated with nightmares. Nevertheless, lucid dream nightmares are decidedly less horrifying than conventional nightmares due to the dreamer's ability to exert a certain level of control over the experience.

In the event that one experiences a harrowing dream while in a state of lucidity, it is worth noting that, unlike conventional apparitions, the individual possesses the ability to retain consciousness of the dream nature. Typically, when one undergoes an unsettling encounter, it becomes difficult to discern it from actuality. In the realm of a lucid dream, one's heightened consciousness affords them the opportunity to acknowledge and proclaim, "I find myself within the confines of a dream." I am merely imagining this. Skilled practitioners of lucid dreaming possess the ability to transform their nightmarish experiences into pleasant and captivating imagery.

In the event of encountering a hostile entity within the realm of a lucid dream, one may opt to allow said unkind entity to engage in an attack, thereby affording oneself the opportunity to observe and analyze the ensuing outcome, taking into account the inherent understanding that all elements within this dream state are of one's own creation. Furthermore, the occurrence of nightmares during lucid dreaming presents a valuable chance to confront anxieties, harness bravery, and effectively cope with adverse emotions.

When a clear dream is transformed into a dreadful experience, our consciousness and ability to exert influence become compromised, despite their prior existence. Similar to all nightmares, the likelihood of experiencing such an event is amplified when one's stress level surpasses normal thresholds. If individuals have undergone traumatic experiences, they may possibly encounter vivid nightmares.

Conversely, in a study conducted, it was found that college students experienced an improved emotional state approximately 60% of the time when they became aware of their dreams during nightmares.

Lucidity was found to significantly enhance the alleviation of nightmares, with a likelihood ratio of seven times higher for improvement as compared to exacerbation. Therefore, when experiencing a nightmare, the potentially improbable and extraordinary occurrences could trigger a sense of clarity, thereby aiding in the resolution of fear and underlying matters associated with it.

Maintaining authentic emotions such as sorrow, anguish, or distress.

Adverse emotional experiences may manifest during a dreaming state, akin to the realities we encounter in our waking existence. It is discernible that one is in a dream during the early stages of dreaming, however, exerting control over the dream may still pose significant challenges. Consequently, you will not exert full command over it, thus potentially compromising the quality of your lucid experience.

Utilizing lucid dreaming as a means of transcending reality.

Escapism can be defined as a purposeful act of disengaging from and diverting one's attention away from the tangible realities of life. If one employs lucid dreaming as a means to disengage from reality, it is unlikely to yield any adverse effects. Nevertheless, engaging in escapism can be beneficial when practiced within societal conventions.

Nevertheless, excessive engagement in such activities may impede both your productivity and hinder personal development. Therefore, in employing lucid dreaming as a means to detach oneself from reality and derive pleasure, it is imperative that one exercises caution and establishes boundaries to prevent it from becoming excessive.

Alternatively, failing to do so could potentially result in disillusionment with one's actual existence, leading to a tendency to solely function within the realm of one's imagination, wherein aspirations and vigor are directed solely towards an illusory realm rather than actuality.

This apprehension often receives considerable media attention and is perhaps the primary factor contributing to people's unease about lucid dreaming. Similar to any endeavor that provides an avenue for individuals to detach themselves from the real world, it has the potential to engender addiction in individuals who struggle with their ability to cope with reality. In contrast to other forms of addiction, lucid dreaming can be readily ceased.

For numerous individuals who experience lucid dreams, the capacity to discern actuality from the realm of dreams does not pose a challenge. Individuals who pursue lucid dreaming as a profession, such as authors, teachers, and public speakers, are able to effectively manage their time between the realms of wakefulness and dreams without experiencing a sense of disorientation.

Certain individuals who are afflicted with mental health disorders may encounter challenges in differentiating between the realms of reality and their dream state. If you are afflicted with a mental disorder or grappling with other forms of addiction, it is advisable to seek guidance from a qualified psychologist prior to embarking on the pursuit of lucid dreaming. The likelihood of experiencing wakefulness while believing to be in a dream state is relatively low, yet it could potentially manifest in individuals with specific mental ailments. If one is pursuing lucid dreaming with the intention of self-exploration or purely as an enthralling pastime, the likelihood of realizing this possibility is slim.

Does succumbing to death within a dream have the capacity to result in mortality outside the realm of the dream?

The notion of perishing in a dream is a source of trepidation among a significant number of individuals. Rest assured, you need not be concerned, as it is an undeniable fact that experiencing death within a lucid dream does not pose any actual risks, owing to the absence of genuine perils associated with the practice of lucid dreaming. It is unquestionably feasible to experience mortal demise during one's slumber or within the realm of dreams. Therefore, the notion that perishing in a dream equates to actual demise is merely a fallacious belief.

Regardless of the exhilaration accompanying the experience of lucid dreaming, it remains an undeniable fact that it is essentially a figment of one's imagination. There is insufficient evidence to support the notion that mortal outcomes can be experienced within the context of a lucid dream. Ultimately, there is little disparity between a lucid dream and a typical dream. It entails a state of consciousness in which one possesses a distinct awareness of being in a dream. How does one potentially face mortality while cognizant that they exist within a realm of slumber, confined solely to the confines of their own psyche?

Indeed, in actuality, should one meet demise while in a state of conscious awareness within a dream, one shall ultimately find oneself awakening unharmed within the confines of one's own bed or within an alternative dream realm. Nevertheless, the most common result is that of awakening.

Numerous individuals have relayed their experiences wherein they have encountered dreams depicting their own demise. The vision of mortality can provide profound insights into existence, renewal, and transcendence. Studies indicate that engaging in lucid dreaming presents a valuable opportunity to confront one's existential apprehensions regarding mortality.

Is it possible to experience apprehension within the confines of a lucid dream?

The notion of being ensnared within an eternal reverie is purely within the realm of speculative literature, feasible solely within the confines of cinematic portrayals. Nevertheless, acquiring consciousness within a dream, wherein one is unable to exert control or awaken from it – connotatively implying a sense of being trapped in the dream state – is an occurrence that should not cause any apprehension.

This concern is unfounded due to the fact that, as previously stated, lucid dreams share many similarities with regular dreams, except for their heightened intensity.

Certain individuals harbor concerns about becoming ensnared within their lucid dream, rendering them incapable of rousing themselves and returning to the realm of reality. However, it is important to note that this scenario has not occurred in any instance. Conversely, the fear frequently arises from an occurrence known as a "false awakening," wherein a conscious dreamer endeavours to rouse themselves only to discover that they are still entrenched in the realm of dreams. Subsequently, after awakening once more, the individual experiencing lucid dreaming realizes that their state of dreaming persists. This pattern has the potential to persist until the individual can regain a firm grasp on actuality.

This captivating occurrence can elicit fear, but it also presents a chance to delve into an alternate realm. Resisting the aforementioned pattern is probable to yield further instances of incorrect perceptions of awakening, yet surrendering to it and acknowledging the state of lucid dreaming can unlock a myriad of potentialities to be examined.

You needn't fear being confined; therefore, embrace the opportunity to demonstrate your capacity to exert control over your surroundings. You shall eventually rouse, as is the case during each period of slumber.

You can have full confidence in the fact that each individual who experiences lucid dreaming has returned to the security of their own sleeping quarters upon awakening. One can acquire the ability to lucid dream at will, thereby enabling conscious awakening. By shutting your eyes tightly and vocalizing with emphasis, "AWAKEN!" you will possess the ability to rouse yourself from the state of dreaming.

Is there a possibility of developing dependence on lucid dreaming?

In certain isolated and exceptional instances, individuals may experience a sense of reliance on the occurrence of lucid dreams. Nevertheless, lucid dreams do not generally foster a dependency among the majority of individuals. For instance, if one were to terminate the lucid dream, the sensation of an uncontrollable psychological yearning or an insuppressible addictive inclination to engage in repeated episodes of lucid dreaming would cease to prevail.

Indubitably, the experience of lucid dreaming brings great delight, and it is only natural to develop a strong inclination to engage in it repeatedly; nevertheless, this does not imply an inability to abstain from it.

Engaging in lucid dreaming can be likened to a recreational pursuit. It is a source of exhilaration, and there exists the potential for desiring heightened levels of lucid dreaming engagement. Nevertheless, this will not transform you into a fervent devotee of lucid dreaming, unless you commence devoting a significant portion of your daylight hours to slumber for the sole purpose of experiencing lucid dreaming.

THAT might be dangerous.

Could lucid dreaming have an impact on the quality of my sleep? Are they tiresome?

Imagine a scenario in which you experience a vivid dream characterized by the sensation of soaring through the air, engaging in energetic movement, and exploring your surroundings. During sleep, our muscles undergo a state of paralysis, rendering physical energy exhaustion illogical in light of the mental activities that transpire.

However, what about the notion of cognitive fatigue? An investigation delved into the apprehensions regarding the potential consequences of frequent lucid dreaming on the quality of sleep.

One may experience fatigue upon awakening if they have indulged in lengthy, numerous, remarkably vivid, and dynamically engaging lucid (or non-lucid) dreaming experiences. Due to the vividness of your dreams, it is plausible that you may encounter difficulty in returning to sleep, potentially leading to sleep deprivation. Nevertheless, particularly in the case of dreams that evoke strong emotions or anxieties, engaging in enjoyable activities is possible when one experiences a lucid dream and exercises control over it. Conversely, the likelihood of encountering psychologically distressing dreams is negligible.

If one continues to be unable to exert control over the dream, it is plausible to encounter emotionally depleting dream experiences, even in a state of lucidity.

Additionally, it should be noted that certain methodologies require individuals to incorporate nocturnal periods and perform the tasks accordingly. The expenditure of energy required to engage in a lucid dream can result in fatigue. Therefore, exercise caution and prudence when employing any of these methods should you choose to experiment with them. Frequently practicing lucid dream techniques that require waking up in the middle of the night can potentially disrupt your sleep patterns.

If one obtains less than 7 hours of sleep, it is possible to experience sleep deprivation, rendering these techniques suboptimal.

Additionally, there exist individuals who possess the inherent ability to effortlessly and consistently experience lucid dreams, commonly referred to as "perma-lucid dreamers" or "natural lucid dreamers". They engage in conscious dreaming every night, assuming it is a universal experience. One might perceive this as being distinctive and perhaps even skillful. However, there are individuals who frequently express their dissatisfaction with feelings of fatigue and being overwhelmed. This is due to the fact that they experience lucid dreaming on a nightly basis. As a result, they are unable to disengage their minds during nighttime.

They are incapable of obtaining sufficient rest.

Although we briefly discussed the importance of exercising caution with regards to sleep deprivation, it is worth noting that numerous individuals who engage in lucid dreaming report feeling rejuvenated and alert following a successful dream exploration.

Engaging in self-discovery, embarking on novel journeys, and indulging in imaginative realms can prove to be invigorating and invigorating.

Given that lucid dreaming occurs during the rapid eye movement (REM) sleep stage, the body and mind are afforded the necessary rest to sustain normal functioning in daily activities. Nevertheless, it appears that the consciousness of the dream state does not significantly impact the majority of individuals.

Occasionally, engaging in the practice of lucid dreaming can prove to be a tiring pursuit. In the event such circumstances arise, simply reduce the duration of your endeavors to engage in lucid dreaming. As an illustration, endeavor to obtain uninterrupted sleep for an entire night on a daily basis, and subsequently make an effort to engage in lucid dreaming multiple times a week during periods of rest.

This will effectively prevent any potential occurrence of sleep deprivation that you may encounter. Regrettably, this subject remains inadequately investigated, hence the absence of empirically supported conclusions.

Therefore, the culmination of these factors leads to the conclusion that dreams, whether lucid or non-lucid, characterized by heightened emotional intensity, perplexity, and psychological disruptions, can result in fatigue and mental exhaustion.

Uncertainty regarding the veracity of a recollection, whether it pertains to a dream or actuality.

This is an infrequent phenomenon. Nevertheless, it is a conceivable occurrence, particularly for individuals diagnosed with borderline personality disorder or similar psychiatric conditions. These psychological conditions will hinder the ability to distinguish between dreams and reality, and it is plausible that the practice of lucid dreaming contributes to the augmentation of confusion between the two states.

If you apprehend potential challenges in distinguishing between dreams and reality, employing a dream journal serves as an ideal practice. Recording your aspirations can serve as a perpetual reminder in discerning events occurring within the realm of imagination and actual occurrences, thus serving as a remarkable method to differentiate between recollections originating from dreams and those derived from reality.

Final Thoughts

The likelihood of these lucid dreaming myths and risks materializing is highly improbable. However, they are possible. If one finds themselves in a state of optimal physical and mental well-being, there should be no cause for concern regarding the occurrence of such phenomena.

Your current location demonstrates an awareness of these risks, ensuring that you will be thoroughly equipped. Subsequently, should you come across them, you will discern the situation and possess the knowledge to determine the appropriate course of action.

If one encounters these unfavorable circumstances repeatedly, it is imperative to introspect and identify the underlying causes, leading to a temporary suspension of pursuit towards one's aspirations.

Overcoming Boundaries within the Realm of Lucid Dreaming

Attaining a state of lucidity in dreaming merely marks the commencement of a lucid dreaming experience. One can begin to release the myriad of constraints and convictions that we bring forth into the realm of dreams through heightened lucid encounters. What is the necessity of engaging in locomotion within the realm of dreaming? What is preventing me from engaging in teleportation? Why am I limited to perceiving only what is ahead of me while being unable to perceive what is behind me, despite the absence of reliance on actual physical visual organs? Why am I incapable of possessing a comprehensive visual field spanning 360 degrees, allowing for simultaneous and complete vision in all directions? What factors are preventing me from ascending and maneuvering through the air like the fictional character Superman? The correct response entails the existence of restrictive mental attitudes and beliefs. In the realm of consciousness, there exist established principles that govern our surroundings. In the realm of dreams, regulations exist as well, albeit in a remarkably flexible manner that essentially enables boundless possibilities. The initial constraints pose the greatest challenge to overcome. I dedicated an extensive amount of time to acquire the skill of flying. Initially, I would experience hesitation in my heart and inevitably encounter a resounding force that would promptly halt my progress. Subsequently, I would initiate flight; however, my lower extremities would remain in contact with the earth's surface, impeding my ability to gain elevation. It required numerous endeavors conducted over a span of several months until achieving the capability to engage in flight.

The dream in which I experienced my inaugural flight was quite comical. I found myself amidst the picturesque countryside hills reminiscent of Switzerland, where a grand, vibrant hot air balloon stood gracefully in a neighboring field. I approached the location and observed the presence of an individual donning a top hat in close proximity to it. I inquired about the purpose of the balloon, to which he responded, "It is meant for you, undoubtedly!" Subsequently, he unlocked the door to the basket, where we both stepped inside. The individual adorned in an uppermost hat proceeded to disengage the tethering cords, leading to our subsequent elevation, just a few feet above ground level. He requested that I grasp the handle and exert upward force to facilitate elevation. I operated the lever, eliciting the emergence of a substantial blaze accompanied by a resonant sound, leading to a gradual ascension in altitude. After exerting force on the handle for a considerable period of time, we eventually ascended into the ethereal domain of the sky. The countryside was beautiful. There were modest dwellings emanating smoke from their chimneys. At a particular juncture, the gentleman adorned with a top hat directed his attention towards me and remarked, "You are aware that this experience bears semblance to the act of aviating, correct?" "Excuse me?" I said. He went on to ask, "In your opinion, what is the nature of this hot air balloon?" It serves merely as a representation for the cognitive faculties of the individual. You are the primary obstacle impeding our progress here, rather than any external factor. I was astonished by his assertion; yet concurrently, a revelation occurred in my mind. He was correct; there is no reason to expect that traversing this environment in a hot air balloon would be any distinct from my hypothetical ability to fly like Superman. Upon my comprehension of the situation, he promptly remarked, "Ah, excellent, now you grasp it," and proceeded to forcefully strike my chest, causing me to be forcefully ejected from the basket. I descended a distance of approximately 30 feet before coming to a stationary position. I had never experienced such an immense sense of liberation before. I harbored some trepidation about attempting to move, as I dreaded the prospect of stumbling, however, I had mastered the art of suspending myself in position. The gentleman donning a top hat vociferated in my direction. "Kindly imagine that you are operating the lever of the hot air balloon, and commence at once!" And obediently, I followed suit. I proceeded towards one of the rural residences emitting smoke from its chimney, whereupon I envisioned operating the lever of the hot air balloon within my thoughts and perceived the familiar resound of combustion. However, this time, I found myself propelled in the desired direction. The indescribable delight, liberation, and excitement I experienced while soaring through the atmosphere are difficult to put into words. The sensation of the wind, the velocity, the uninhibited sense of freedom were truly remarkable. It appears that the gentleman adorned in formal attire deemed it necessary to impart a stern lesson by expelling me from the gondola, a gesture for which I remained profoundly appreciative.

Expanding boundaries within the realm of Lucid dreaming can also be harnessed for practical applications. I have a handful of acquaintances within the scientific community who utilize the practice of Lucid dreaming as a strategy to develop and refine ideas and concepts. Undoubtedly, not all applications need to possess such virtuous intent. On a previous occasion, I deliberately initiated a state of lucid dreaming in order to familiarize myself with a video game that I intended to engage in during a social gathering with acquaintances. It was very effective.

The concept regarding Lucid dreaming lies in its profound connection to one's emotive state. Merely because it is a reverie does not imply that you ought to engage in unrestricted behavior. Any action undertaken within a state of lucid dreaming is bound to evoke an emotional response. It appears that exhibiting kindness and showing respect towards others holds equal significance in the realm of dreams as it does in the tangible world. Overcoming restrictions within Lucid dreams is predominantly an emotional rather than a mental experience. In the instance of my endeavor to acquire the skill of flying, it was evident that I possessed a clear and vivid comprehension of my desire to achieve flight. However, I had not fully relinquished the belief on an emotional level. It was solely through the acceptance of my emotions that I found the ability to soar, albeit accompanied by physical encouragement from a companion.

At times, achieving remarkable feats in semi-lucid or Aware dreams can prove to be less challenging compared to their counterpart, Lucid dreams. Certain lucid dreams exhibit a higher degree of thought responsiveness compared to others, as this is inherent within the realm of dreaming. Dream environments can be employed in a myriad of ways, yet it is important to recognize that the absence of constraints does not imply that one should forsake all limitations. Similar to the progression that led to your exploration of Lucid dreams, allow the organic transformation of shedding constraints to ensue gradually as you gradually broaden your perspectives.

Overcoming Limitations in Lucid Dreaming

- It is an inherent aspect of lucid dreaming that the constraints one possesses regarding life are inherently transferred and manifested within the realm of these dreams.

It will demand a considerable amount of time and effort to gradually overcome your limitations and fully embrace the myriad possibilities that Lucid dreams offer.

- Lucid dreams demonstrate a strong connection with one's emotions, thus endeavor to bring about emotional transformations in beliefs rather than solely relying on cognitive processes.
- Display kindness and respect towards all dream characters and circumstances, as they are symbolic representations of the self within your dreams.

Establishing an Ideal Haven

Dreaming, in its multifaceted manifestations, has the potential to profoundly transform our lives. However, if your aspirations involve maintaining your existing life circumstances while seeking a more comfortable financial situation and resolution of emotional turmoil, this particular path may not yield the desired outcome.

Manda Scott

Due to the fact that this chapter elucidates a methodology pertaining to the establishment of a dream sanctuary, it is imperative that we grasp the contextual framework underlying this concept, namely Shamanism.

Manda Scott, a British author, demonstrates a fervent fascination with Shamanism and the associated rituals. As she articulately expresses, "Shamanic practice represents the contemporary manifestation of indigenous spiritual traditions." As previously deliberated in the preceding chapter, spirit guides originate from precisely the identical origin.

I concur with Scott's viewpoint, which brings forth an important observation: the fascination of the Western world with Shamanism should not be taken as definitive proof of the absolute veracity of its original expression. However, as I have also previously indicated, it is our collective responsibility to investigate and examine this matter. And this, Scott, should be done with mindfulness, as we all should strive to do.

Let us now turn our attention to the exploration of enhancing the immersive experience of a dream sanctuary by introducing an element of depth through an examination of Shamanism and the intricate connection it holds with the concept of the dream sanctuary.

Shamanism's 3 Pillars

Shamanic dreaming is comprised of three aspects: conventional dreaming, lucid dreaming, and waking dreams (the state of full consciousness in everyday life, in contrast to the state of lucidity).

This form of dreaming constitutes an integral component of the tripartite framework employed in Shamanic traditions. A ritual is among those that commonly accompany dreams. Ritual practice entails the tangible and grounded utilization of material elements within the physical realm. This practice grounds the individual in actuality, sanctifying the intangible through the holy substance as prescribed by the Divine.

The practice of ritual is founded upon the correlation between the four cardinal directions and the four points on the compass. This aligns the cardinal directions and compass points with the four fundamental elements: earth, air, water, and fire. The sensual nature of Shamanic ritualism is replicated in discernible ways across the various indigenous cultures that subsist worldwide. The immaterial bestows sacredness upon the material through mutual reciprocity within an everlasting cycle of rejuvenation. The existence of one is contingent upon the presence of the other within this realm of spirituality. Just as the unity of body and spirit exists, so too does the inseparability of the tangible and intangible aspects. There is not the slightest shred of a veil, no matter how tenuous. Everything is merely a singular entity. And all are accessible.

There exists no inflexible manner in which to ceremonially convey Shamanism. It rests within the discretion of the practitioner, as it does within the realm of every religious belief, notwithstanding the firm grip of rigid doctrine.

The ultimate component of Shamanism is indisputably Shamanic journeying, an integral undertaking within the realm of Shamanism. Through the rhythmic pulsation of the percussion instrument, the adept embarks upon an experiential journey to the myriad dimensions of existence, encountering esteemed mentors, ethereal beings, animals of wisdom, and the celestial entities that dwell therein.

The essence of shamanism lies in achieving a state of union with the entirety of existence, including the concealed realms of all realities, much like the essence of Buddhism. Attaining unity requires overcoming the troublesome dichotomy prevailing in Western society, which segregates humans, animals, and other entities into distinct groups with varying degrees of significance. This behavior is outweighed by its negative consequences, and Shamanism aims to remedy it. However, Shamanism is not recognized or practiced in Western societies.

Scott's argument is that the concept of a Shaman does not exist within Western society. The rationale behind this can be attributed to the core principles of Shamanism, which include:

• The Art of Living • Strategies for a Fulfilling Life • A Guide to Life's Journey

Shamanism is dedicated to the practice of mindfulness and recognizes the importance of experiencing each moment with profound appreciation and gratitude. This constitutes the art of living, refraining from incessantly pursuing wealth and all the associated desires and ambitions that come with it. Instead, existence entails serving as an integral participant in all that transpires.

• Methods of Mortality • Approaches to Ceasing One's Existence • A Guide to the Conclusion of Life

The essential principle here is humility, serving as a substitute for the Western fixation on incentives and penalties. It is an inherent aspect of our existence! Through fully embracing the unfolding of the world in every passing moment of our lives, we approach the inevitability of death with a sense of serene composure.

Through adopting a stance of humbleness when confronted with mortality, we relinquish our excessive desire for absolute certainty and guarantees. There is neither recompense nor penalty. Death exists without reason, and our understanding of its significance remains elusive. All of our endeavors to portray it as a menace to the living prove to be fruitless. The various afterlives that are assured to us after death solely depict our own insatiable longings rather than any discernible veracity. Modesty is the quality that enables us to navigate the confines of our own ambitious and discontented selves.

These two reasons represent the main impediments to the existence of Shamans within a Western framework. This society inherently lacks the capacity to embrace qualities such as humility or mindfulness. Our thought processes are excessively aligned with the notions of conflict and domination, dichotomies and self-actualization, rendering them unsuitable for harmonious coexistence with Shamanistic practices.

The Significance of the Dream Sanctuary

A dream sanctuary is a secure haven wherein individuals can convene with their spirit guides, ancestors, and other vivid dream entities, in order to collaborate and carry out meaningful interactions. This is an enduring construction endeavor, requiring a steadfast disposition and unwavering concentration.

Having familiarized yourself with the concept of materializing entities, individuals, and imaginary settings, you are now equipped to establish a secure haven where your visionary mentors may convene with you to discuss pressing and significant matters pertaining to your spiritual, psychological, and overall waking existence.

The crucial aspect here is the establishment of a stable and secure environment. The successful realization of the space relies on meticulous attention to detail. The greater depth of visualization you achieve in envisioning the dream sanctuary, the more steadfast and impenetrable its existence shall become. One could perhaps consider it to be akin to a protective fortress for the essence of one's being. In order to enhance our understanding of the intended function of a dream sanctuary, let us refer to the precise definition of the term to establish a more tangible connection to it within the realm of lucid dreaming.

A sanctuary is a haven that offers solace to individuals in search of security. For the objectives you seek to accomplish, safety is synonymous with the presence of a secure and enduring environment within the realm of dreams, wherein the risk of structural failure is highly improbable. Your envisioned haven is a consecrated realm for the profound exploration of one's inner self. This is a primary factor that necessitates the cultivation of connections with your spiritual guides through the act of extending oneself with modesty and affability. The necessity of your spirit guides' presence lies in the fact that they thrive when their assistance is required. This need serves as a key objective, aiming to establish a sacred connection with your dreams in order to derive great value from the ancestral knowledge bestowed by your spirit guides.

Taking all of these factors into consideration, it is now appropriate to shift our attention towards the physical space itself and the specific attributes that it must possess in order to effectively cater to your requirements.

A Hiding Place

As a result of its intended function, your dream sanctuary stands out as a distinctive aspect of lucid dreaming. This phenomenon remains unchanged in your vivid dream realm, and it may require a considerable amount of time for you to attain sufficient mastery in materializing this environment as a reliable occurrence within your lucid dreams.

By engaging in a process of pre-fabrication, you are effectively constructing a mental image or symbol. The greater the level of stability it possesses within your psyche, the greater the level of stability it shall manifest within your lucid dreams. This is precisely why attention to detail holds utmost significance. Devote some time to contemplate the types of environments in which you experience a sense of security and emotional nourishment. It is possible that your desired personal retreat could manifest as either a cavern nestled within a rocky facade or a tent resembling the traditional dwellings of the Bedouin people. The initial aspect that should be taken into consideration is whatever the concept of "safety" represents to individual perspectives.

Take, for instance, consider the places that held the strongest allure during your childhood. I recollect being present inside the automobile while my family journeyed towards a nearby urban center. The central divider of the highway was adorned with green grass, punctuated by occasional clusters of evergreen trees, shrubs, and bushes at their foot. As we traversed these areas, I would invariably indulge in fantasies of inhabiting the idyllic arboreal surroundings. I envisioned myself ensconced within a tent, adorned with plush cushions and luxurious Afghans. One other cherished area of interest comprised the artifact known as the genie bottle in the well-regarded television series, I Dream of Jeannie. I have consistently harbored a desire to reside within that exquisite bottle, adorned with its captivating decor and opulent cushions.

Although childhood dreams may appear frivolous in the eyes of adults, they offer valuable insights into our underlying psychological requirements. As a child, being an introvert, I had a tendency to conceal myself. I found the concept of being present in visible surroundings yet maintaining invisibility quite intriguing. Devote a certain amount of time to contemplating your childhood concealment spots and the rationale behind your selection. What was the purpose of your visit to that location? What were your sentiments during your visit to them?

Meaningful Surroundings

After determining your perception of safety and comfort within your sacred dream space, it becomes imperative to contemplate the desired aesthetic of the space. Please bear in mind that this is a permanent endeavor. The dream sanctuary is deliberately designed to be unchanging and secure, as this is the optimal setting for addressing existential inquiries, engaging in dialogue with your spirit guides, and uncovering the insights they have to offer.

I firmly adhere to the belief in the profound influence of color. This holds particular significance for your desired haven, as the chosen hue invariably establishes the ambiance of a space. It conveys a pronounced message concerning the intended purpose and atmosphere. Select hues that resonate with your inner self and appreciate the profound symbolism associated with the colors you are selecting. Color evokes a resonating quality and possesses a distinct energetic essence. Kindly take into account these hues and their metaphysical significance:

- Green: It represents the hue found abundantly in the natural environment, embodying equilibrium and the fostering of seamless interaction. It is perfect for creating a tranquil haven in whichever hue desired.
- The color yellow encompasses reason, while also embodying elements of enjoyment, intellect, and personal empowerment.
- Orange: This vibrant hue possesses the ability to stimulate energy levels, enhance work output, and inspire innovative problem-solving approaches. Please note that the proposed concept

may have an excess of vibrancy for a traditional dream sanctuary.

- The color red represents physical vitality and passion, evoking spontaneity while also conveying a sense of stability. Exercise restraint when incorporating this color into your design. It will aid in the stabilization of the space; however, excessive presence of it within your dream sanctuary might impede communication.

Purple: This profoundly spiritual hue proves to be perfectly suited for creating a dream-saturated haven. Select a gem-hued shade to enhance your envisioned area, invoking a sense of heightened intuition and the vibrant energies of the cosmos coursing within.

- Azure: An exquisite hue of blue, possessing a deep and vibrant quality, will harmoniously enhance the visual and emotional allure of your complementary color palette. Signifying peace, love, emotional profundity, and spiritual openness, blue is a natural fit for your dream sanctuary.

Please take into account the purpose of the dream sanctuary and how you intend it to function in your state of lucid dreaming, when considering your preferred colors. Careful consideration should be given to the selection of colors, followed by their harmonious application, in order to establish a space that brings delight to both the visual senses and the inner being, thereby fostering the intended purpose of the sanctuary.

Taking Care

What is the significance of color in your envisioned sanctuary of dreams? Every color possesses a profound spiritual resonance. Every hue instills within us a distinct emotional response. The phenomenon of color exerts influence, as does the field of design. This is particularly accurate when selecting colors for your ideal sanctuary based on their resonance with you, and crafting the space to cater to the distinct requirements of your soul.

As you advance in the pursuit of establishing your ideal sanctuary, it is crucial to contemplate your desires and aspirations. You are not adhering to any prescribed format or template, irrespective of the origin or tradition of the practice. You adeptly establish the exact spatial confines necessary, employing the appropriate methodology, in order to solidify it as an unchanging constituent within your vivid dreams. You are establishing this sanctified environment in order to seek solace for your soul, in the company of individuals who possess the greatest capacity to assist you in fulfilling those spiritual requirements. There shall be no deviation in the visual aspects of this realm within your dreams. It is of utmost importance that it remains consistently accessible to you in the exact manner as it has been in any previous dream. This is a mental sanctuary that must maintain its steadfastness and preparedness to serve you, providing guidance, facilitating dialogue, and providing solutions to any inquiries that emerge during the course of lucid dreaming or in the realm of wakefulness. This platform serves as an invaluable resource for exploring the concept of lucid dreaming, facilitating personal growth, and fostering spiritual development by connecting individuals with their guiding spirits, be it ancestral entities, archetypal figures, or individuals who may seem unfamiliar yet oddly recognizable.

Thus, exercise caution while choosing the components of your ideal sanctuary. Please keep in mind that you are creating a revered environment intended solely for your personal utilization. Recognizing the sanctity of your human journey necessitates acknowledging the same sanctity within your soul. Ensure that you possess a clear understanding of your inherent value. If you are unable to affirm your knowledge of that, it signifies that you need to engage in some restorative practices before undertaking any endeavor as intricate, rigorous, and enlightening as the establishment of a reverie haven.

And that, without question, is not a negative aspect. Every aspect of existence is centered around progress and development. Once growth ceases, mortality takes hold. Despite any unexpected incidents, a lack of progress indicates the impending culmination of the human existence.

This occurrence is not rooted in the absence of worth or lack of "productivity" (as our contemporary preoccupation suggests). Rather, it arises from the organism regressing and instigating a state of overall disorder.

Whether due to negligence, self-inflicted harm, illness, unforeseen events such as accidents or acts of terrorism, or the natural occurrence of passing away during our rest, mortality is an inevitable outcome. However, when we relinquish all opportunities for personal development, we merely exist as lifeless vessels, carrying out actions devoid of purpose - akin to being in a state of spiritual decay.

Thus, the concept of growing edges can be regarded as a means of guidance as well. We all have them, and we should all welcome them as the wonderful outfall of being these incredible speaking, cognitively advanced beings we are.

Techniques Of Lucid Dreaming

The phenomenon of lucid dreaming has been verified through scientific research, establishing its existence and demonstrating that individuals from all walks of life can potentially experience it. Each experiment conducted by esteemed sleep or dream experts within laboratory settings. Through a systematic series of experiments, a set of methodologies were devised with the intended purpose of facilitating individuals' attainment of lucid dreaming.

Nevertheless, lucid dreaming is not artificially developed in laboratories. This particular discipline was observed and adhered to by various religious and spiritual practitioners globally since antiquity, including Monks, Sufis, Shamans, Mystics, Yogis, and

Spiritualists. The techniques were possessed by them. However, today you will be introduced to novel laboratory-developed terminologies and methodologies that are, to some extent, more streamlined and efficient. We express our gratitude to the dedicated professionals in the laboratories.

The technique known as Mnemonic Induction of Lucid Dreams (MILD)

This methodology was devised by Dr. Stephen LaBerge during the pursuit of his doctoral degree. It encompasses four distinct procedural stages. The significance of this technique hinges on your capacity to commit your previous dreams to memory in order to generate or elicit subsequent dreams. Let's take a look.

Documenting and Retrieving the Dream Experience

During this particular stage, it is necessary for you to have a dream journal in close proximity to your sleeping area. Upon awakening from slumber, make it a practice to record on paper any recollections you may have from the dream. Take note of the specific date and time, and, if needed, attempt to create a rudimentary depiction of any significant details from the dream, even if you possess limited artistic abilities.

The recollection of every dream is not always possible. The majority of dreams lack sufficient vividness, thereby impeding the retention of any significant visual content they may contain. If one has no recollection of a dream, it is possible that no dream occurred.

Prior to the present moment, you may peruse your notes in order to ascertain its relevance to your current physiological, psychological, or environmental state. For instance, it is conceivable that you shall observe a correlation between the contents of your dream and the distressing encounter that you have recently undergone. Alternatively, one could consider observing the events that unfold in the following days subsequent to the dream, whereby it is conceivable to interpret these occurrences as a tangible reflection of the dream. While there may appear to be no discernible connection to lucid dreaming, it will serve to convince your subconscious that the occurrence of a notable event will precipitate the onset of dreaming.

Reality Checks

Reality checks are techniques employed to enhance one's cognitive acuity in discerning between actual reality and the realm of dreams. Undoubtedly, we typically possess an understanding of the distinction. Nevertheless, during episodes of dreaming, such actions are not typically performed. In the realm of the dream, all elements lie beyond the realm of our conscious awareness, thus precluding us from discerning the distinction between reality and the realm of the dream.

A reality assessment should be conducted during the state of dreaming. Ensure that you remain aware of your state of consciousness during the act of dreaming. That is the point. However, you need to build a habit of reality check so that you can do it easily in the dream. Unless you cultivate this behavior regularly, it will not be manifested within your subconscious mind during your sleep.

Lucid dreamers propose the method of gently brushing the wall surface with your palm or fingertip while simultaneously focusing your intention on the progressive penetration of the finger through the wall. In actuality, this occurrence is not feasible, but within the realm of imagination, it is indeed possible. With an increase in your perceptual consciousness of reality, there will consequently be a commensurate augmentation in your cognizance of the dream realm.

Should this behavior become ingrained, it will be executed with relative ease during the state of slumber. The achievement of experiencing lucid dreaming can be attributed to one's recognition of being in a dream state. Naturally, there are alternative methods to verify reality, such as engaging in mathematical exercises, observing one's reflection in a mirror, or applying a controlled level of heat to one's fingertip.

However, it is important to note that I do not advise the latter approach.

Lucid Affirmations

Convince your subconscious mind of a state of dreaming, even in the absence of an actual dream. As one immerses oneself in a state of rest and repose upon the mattress, sporadic visions may manifest. In the event of such occurrences, it is advisable to internally affirm the notion that "I am currently engaged in a state of dreaming" or "the subsequent perception will manifest as a dream."

If you persist in engaging in this behavior deliberately, your subconscious mind is inclined to carry it out as an authoritative directive. Imagine that you have reached the state of readiness to drift into slumber. Should your directive be duly acknowledged and acted upon by the subconscious mind, you shall seamlessly transition into a subsequent realm or visualization known as a dream. Nevertheless, that does not constitute the culmination of this method. According to popular belief, if one finds themselves in the hypnagogic state characterized by the vivid emergence of random visions, one should proceed with the fourth step in order to successfully enter the state of an ideal lucid dream.

Dream Visualization

Occasionally, novice individuals overlook this particular step due to their rapid tendency to fall asleep. This does not pertain to the act of envisioning a dream while in a state of wakefulness. This is elicited when one is on the periphery of the transitional state between wakefulness and slumber. In the realm of "human" communication, such a state is achieved by one's physical and mental relaxation, wherein the random visual manifestations become exceptionally vivid. These two conditions are imperative.

In order to effectively manifest a desired outcome, it is imperative to engage in the imaginative process, mentally placing oneself within the envisioned scenario. Do not confine the scope of your imaginative visualization within a singular viewpoint. Ensure the incorporation of your additional sensors. An illustration of this would be that merely envisioning a location falls short in terms of effective visualization. A more refined approach involves engaging in mental imagery whereby you envision yourself present within the aforementioned location.

Upon reaching that state, one becomes cognizant of being in a dream, which constitutes the essence of lucid dreaming: the fundamental realization of one's current state as a dream.

How does MILD work?

It could be observed that those steps are not intrinsically interconnected. It appears that the attainment of lucid dreaming may be facilitated by a mere couple of sequential actions. However, it is not. Allow me to provide an explanation on the functioning of this.

Dreams are phenomenological occurrences that possess the capacity to be recollected. Nevertheless, in order to recollect the dreams, it is imperative to retain the imprints of the dream in our memory. Recognizing a dream signifies our cognizance of the existence of dreams. Nevertheless, recalling dreams can prove challenging unless the dreams manifest themselves in a particularly vivid manner. In order to retain recollections of dreams, it is essential to document them in a specific manner. It is of utmost importance to promptly document the contents of one's dream upon awakening, as any delay in doing so may result in the gradual dissipation of the recollection. Engaging in other activities prior to writing stimulates neuronal activity, diverting cognitive resources away from the task at hand. Subsequently, the recollection of your dreams gradually diminishes.

In order to retrieve the dream, it is imperative to possess the capacity to intuit its sensory qualities, including its textures, visual appearance, auditory characteristics, and so forth. We must delineate between the realm of dreaming and reality, hence the necessity for implementing reality checks. The emotion evoked by the dream, distinct from reality, serves as a catalyst to attain the state of lucid dreaming.

Now, equipped with that acquired understanding and emotional resonance of the dream, you proceed to rest and endeavor to recollect it. Nevertheless, it is worth noting that at times, one's subconscious mind may impede the ability to fully encounter such an experience. Your neurological processes adhere to their own governing principles and are not easily subject to interference. It possesses a form of safeguard, positioned at the periphery of the conscious realm, where the boundary between slumber and wakefulness resides. The affirmation functions akin to the directive. Continuously reciting the affirmation is equivalent to queuing the command. Upon entering the state of slumber, the aforementioned instruction shall be carried out foremost by your subconscious cognition.

Once the subconscious mind carries out this directive, it is imperative to provide it with indications that guide its actions, enabling it to direct you accordingly. That is the specific time and place in which your dream visualization becomes effective. Failure to complete this action will result in your subconscious mind manifesting the dream that you recall or document. Nevertheless, you will succumb to an ordinary dream of lesser intensity or lacking the vividness you desire in a lucid dream.

Now, these steps facilitate the execution of an integrated process. Those are interrelated. By purposefully carrying out the prescribed actions, one can attain the state of lucid dreaming. Nevertheless, it does not invariably yield immediate results. Take your time. If achieving lucid dreaming were as effortless as an average dream, Dr. Stephen LaBerge would not have pursued it as the subject of his doctoral studies.

The method of cycle adjustment, also known as the CAT technique.

This methodology was devised by a recognized authority in the realm of lucid dreaming, namely Daniel Love. This methodology is derived from the diurnal sleep cycle. For an adult individual, it is customary to allocate approximately 7 to 8 hours of sleep per night, signifying not the periodicity but rather the total duration. During each night, it is common for individuals to experience 4-5 sleep cycles, wherein they may briefly awaken 4-5 times, despite often being unaware of these awakenings. We consistently experience complete awakening from sleep at least once nightly. Typically, each sleep cycle has a duration of 90 minutes.

It is important to pay attention to the time at which you typically awaken during the night, unrelated to any external disturbances that may disrupt your sleep. As an illustration, if your typical bedtime is 22.00 and you ordinarily arise at 03.00, it would be necessary for you to shift your wake-up time to an earlier hour (such as 02.30) for a minimum duration of one week. Set your alarm on.

Your sleep cycle undergoes a transformation within the span of a week. This practice will condition your subconscious mind to awaken at the precise time of 02.30. Nevertheless, the alteration does not significantly impact your overarching sleep cycle as it necessitates a minimum of 21 days to fully modify it. Fortunately, such is not the modus operandi of the CAT. The Circadian Alteration Technique (CAT) functions by inducing subtle modifications in the sleep cycle, with the objective of potentially disorienting the subconscious mind, in my personal perception. In order to comprehend this, it is imperative that you engage in the task assigned for the second week.

During the second week, you alternate your waking schedule between the standard wake-up time and the CAT wake-up time. As an illustration, consider the following sequence: initially, you awaken at 02.30, followed by awakening at 03.00, then reverting back to 02.30, and subsequently returning to 03.00. You do this daily. Here, you are causing confusion within your subconscious mind. Your inner psyche rouses your consciousness at precisely 02.30, yet you do not awaken until the clock strikes 03.00. Therefore, you will be granted a period of 30 minutes during which you may experience lucid dreaming.

Are you able to perceive the simplicity of this technique? Yes, it is. If you execute this technique with precision, you can anticipate experiencing a minimum of four lucid dreams per week. This phenomenon occurs due to the existence of three regular wake-up times in combination with four times of wakefulness induced by the CAT sessions. The moment at which your subconscious mind rouses you coincides with the period during which you are still in a state of slumber. What is the term for experiencing awakeness during a state of sleep? Thus concludes the phenomenon of lucid dreaming.

Wake Induced Lucid Dreams, commonly referred to as WILD, are a type of altered consciousness state in which individuals achieve lucidity within their dreams by deliberately maintaining awareness during the transition from wakefulness to sleep.

This technique has been cultivated and utilized by Tibetan monks and Yogis for countless centuries, attesting to its immense potency within the realm of lucid dreaming. If you follow the instructions outlined below, you will be able to access lucid dreaming at your convenience. Nevertheless, it is imperative to exercise great caution as one may inadvertently succumb to the phenomenon of astral projection.

One will observe certain resemblances between the WILD and the MILD (as well as the CAT); however, they certainly possess distinct characteristics. If the MILD technique is employed prior to sleep, the WILD technique is employed during the sleep onset period. In order for the Wake-Initiated Lucid Dreaming (WILD) technique to be effective, it is necessary to engage in an initial prolonged period of sleep, followed by a subsequent awakening during which the necessary steps for inducing a second opportunity to sleep should be undertaken. Does it resemble the feline specimen in auditory presentation? Therefore, ensure that you activate your alarm clock.

The key aspect of the Wake-Initiated Lucid Dreaming technique lies in the state wherein your physical body is in slumber while your consciousness remains alert. It means that you need to put your body in total relaxation. In order to achieve this physical condition, the Wake-Induced Lucid Dreaming (WILD) technique is performed subsequent to the completion of several hours of sleep. Typically, our physical state assumes this condition upon waking up. We avail ourselves of this opportunity to partake in the realm of the lucid dream. Here are the steps.

Relaxation

This particular stage is essential when initiating the Wake-Induced Lucid Dreaming technique prior to engaging in any substantial sleep. Recline supine or assume an alternative position that affords comfort. Ensure that you are sufficiently at ease to refrain from shifting or turning on your bed.

Direct your focus towards your breath, which progresses in a profound and unhurried manner. After each exhalation, allow your body to fully relax and sink into the mattress. While maintaining closed eyelids, direct your focus towards darkness, refraining from making judgments or becoming attached to any observable phenomena. Thoughts and images of people and locations may come to your mind, but it is advisable not to exert undue pressure on yourself to expel them. Allow them to freely roam and pursue their own course.

It is imperative not only for your body to attain a state of relaxation, but also for your mind and emotions to achieve the same level of tranquility. You have the option to engage in introspective reflection or recollect the events of the afternoon. Please consider your plans for tomorrow. Induce a state of silence among them. It is most advisable to merely observe their behavior without passing any judgement.

In due course, you shall discern the gradual desensitization of your physical being. Your physical senses perceive a pronounced weightiness that impedes mobility. Nevertheless, refrain from attempting any bodily movement. Please be mindful that your physical being experiences periods of rest. If it becomes essential, endeavor to convince your thought processes that you are in a state of slumber. If you find yourself experiencing an itch, I would advise you to gently alleviate the sensation by scratching the affected area and then initiating a fresh beginning.

During this phase, individuals who possess a proclivity for deep sleep may find themselves rapidly succumbing to slumber. Therefore, adhere to the established plan. Remain vigilant with your thoughts while directing your focus towards the numbing sensation in your physical being. If you keep this on track, you will feel floated and that is good.

Sleep Paralysis

When one's body is in a state of sleep, mobility becomes notably challenging. That is the extent of our current knowledge regarding sleep paralysis. This represents the gateway to your exploration of lucid dreaming as well as astral projection. Nevertheless, when it comes to astral projection, sleep paralysis proves to be the most accessible but also the most unfavorable gateway.

During this stage, it is possible to experience an unfamiliar sensation characterized by a gentle oscillation and audible disturbances. There is no inherent issue with that. If one experiences both the sensation and the auditory stimuli, employing one's imaginative faculties to visualize a particular setting or pleasant auditory ambiance may be beneficial.

When confronted with this situation, it is possible for fear to arise. You may experience unforeseen hallucinations, however, these perceptions are merely products of your cognition. Your apprehension finds expression in the object of your fear. Should those visions manifest, it would suggest that you are currently experiencing a state of dreaming. Alternatively, you can envision your desired scenario.

You might consider repositioning yourself in bed to awaken your body. Nevertheless, that is not the intended course of action. Do not allow apprehension to overshadow your happiness. Stick on the plan.

Many novice individuals find themselves in this state of being trapped, primarily due to specific portions of their physical body remaining alert or lacking in relaxation. Hence, it is imperative to verify if specific areas of your body are still experiencing tension.

Visualizing the Dream Scene

Assuming you find yourself in an optimal state of sleep paralysis, it is likely that you would experience vivid visions at this time. It appears as though various channels intermittently appear and disappear on the television screens. It signifies your preparedness for departure, yet you lack a destination. So, make one.

It is likely to facilitate the process of visualizing the desired dream scene, provided one already possesses knowledge regarding the specific dream they aim to enter. Nevertheless, if you desire to ponder the matter at this juncture, it is belated. Your conscious awareness will assume control and you will regain wakefulness. Consequently, it is imperative to establish the context of the dream scenario prior to commencing it. Your dream journal might prove to be of assistance in this context. You have the capacity to retrieve the dream that you have previously encountered. If you aspire to generate the novel entity, ensure that you possess it beforehand.

For instance, should you aspire to envision yourself atop the Himalayas, it is imperative that you first familiarize yourself with a visual representation of the aforementioned location. Alternatively, you may envision it beforehand. Contemplating the appearance of the Himalayas while experiencing sleep paralysis serves no practical purpose. I have made numerous attempts, resulting in my experience of sleep paralysis and the sensation of floating above my physical self. In due course, I succumb to the phenomenon of astral projection.

I would like to provide a comment pertaining to astral projection through the Wake-Induced Lucid Dreaming technique. The majority of writers incorporate it as an out-of-body experience (OBE) exit method within the context of lucid dreaming. It is not. Upon experiencing astral projection, I proceeded to ascertain whether it was a state of dreaming or not. On a certain day, I embarked upon the task and proceeded to my spouse's work area within her place of employment. I have observed a book pertaining to the subject. The following day, I inquired as to the title of the book resting upon the table. She responded and subsequently verified the veracity of my observations. It is worth mentioning that I have not entered her room (located within the office premises) up to this moment. Astral projection differs from lucid dreaming.

Develop Self-Awareness

Given that you are actively engaging in these exercises and immersing yourself in this book, do you possess a conscious understanding of your own existence? Your thoughts, emotions, and essence shall forever encompass your existence. Consider it as developing an understanding of the self, specifically the concept of "I" or one's ego. You have the ability to perceive, observe, sense, contemplate, inhale, and undergo a wide range of emotions. You are the focal point of your life, around which all occurrences revolve.

Please endeavor to revisit the preceding exercises while directing your attention towards your emotions or individual engagement within each iteration. For instance, when engaging in the 5-4-3-2-1 exercise, refrain from using a plain statement such as "the garden outside." Instead, utilize language that emphasizes your active perception, such as "I observe the presence of the garden outside." Maintain your attention and mindfulness throughout each moment.

Develop a Consciousness of Your Cognizance

Do you perceive yourself experiencing an increased sense of awareness through each exercise? Individuals endowed with an amplified state of consciousness tend to exhibit a heightened degree of reverence for their surroundings, fleeting instances, and the very essence of their lived encounters. Gaining consciousness of one's own awareness facilitates a deeper comprehension of oneself and one's cognitive processes. It provides a framework for establishing your position in relation to other entities and one's self-concept. Awareness enables mind training. One acquires the ability to deliberately activate cognitive states, thus enabling the utilization of the mind's complete capabilities.

Attain a state of self-awareness through the application of the subsequent exercise. Pay a visit to a moderately bustling destination such as a public park or retail complex. Direct your focus towards particular entities or phenomena, such as recognizing individuals, olfactory perceptions, and spatial orientation in relation to surrounding elements. Employ all of your sensory faculties whilst perceiving the surrounding scenery. Direct your attention to a diverse range of stimuli and shift your focus accordingly. Direct your attention to the larger context while also attending to the act of regulating your breath. Develop self-awareness and conscious acknowledgement of your own cognitive states.

Comparing Lucid Dreaming with Reality

What is your perception of these exercises that bear resemblance to lucid dreaming? Much of what you have recently encountered in actuality is also relevant in the realm of dreams. The realm of dreams is replete with diverse multisensory encounters, encompassing visual perceptions, auditory sensations, tactile experiences, cognitive processes, and gustatory impressions. The primary distinction between the realm of dreams and the realm of reality resides in the provenance of the observed perceptions. In the realm of reality, one is subjected to external stimuli, whereas the realm of dreams stems from an internal source.

These encounters can be highly bewildering, prompting individuals to ponder whether they are truly in a state of wakefulness or immersed in a dream-like scenario. In reality, your conscious mind aids in discerning the distinction between actuality and imagination, thereby enabling you to ascertain your current mental state. Typically, dreams impose constraints on one's sensory perception as they predominantly encompass awareness of the immediate vicinity, whereas in wakefulness, one's awareness extends beyond, encompassing sounds from the surrounding environment or beyond the confines of one's immediate location.

On numerous occasions, one may discern their presence in a dream due to the lack of realism exhibited by the imagery and unfolding events. As an illustration, it is plausible that you are present at the seaside without recollecting the manner in which you arrived, or perchance you inhabit a substantial distance away from the coastal regions. An additional illustration pertains to alterations in bodily characteristics, where one might encounter a distorted form or demonstrate the capacity to pass their fingers through their physical frame. An additional illustration involves observing one's surroundings within the dream state in search of elements that defy reality, such as peculiar beings or landscapes. Your conscious mind, whilst in the state of dreaming, possesses a heightened sense of awareness, enabling you to recognize that you are indeed immersed in a dream state rather than perceiving actual reality.

There is often a tendency for the boundaries between dreams and reality to become unclear when individuals undergo episodes of false awakenings. A fabricated reawakening transpires when one emerges from a dream, only to discern that they remain in a state of slumber or effectively imprisoned within a surreal realm, subsequently regaining consciousness in actuality a short while thereafter. Numerous individuals perceive this encounter as disconcerting and harbor concerns regarding the blurring of their dreams and reality, coupled with a perceived inability to extricate themselves from such a state. One of the most disconcerting occurrences of false awakening arises when an individual dreams of getting out of bed, taking a shower, and commencing their daily routine, only to subsequently realize that this scenario is in fact illusory. The act of conducting a reality check is indispensable in this scenario, as it serves the purpose of discerning whether one is experiencing wakefulness or is, indeed, immersed in a state of dreaming through the utilization of conscious awareness.

Advantages of Lucid Dreaming

At this juncture, you ought to possess a more comprehensive understanding of the nature of lucid dreaming. I find myself consistently filled with fervor regarding the concept of lucid dreaming due to its profoundly enchanting nature. The multitude of reasons to engage in lucid dreaming renders it an inherently advantageous practice. One may envision any desired scenario, regardless of its feasibility in practical terms.

Relieves Emotional Distress

Lucid dreaming offers an opportunity to detach oneself from one's everyday existence. It serves as a valuable respite from depression, anxiety, or pervasive feelings of melancholy. Numerous individuals who encounter insomnia, characterized by the challenge of initiating or maintaining sleep during nighttime, discover that engaging in lucid dreaming offers them a source of anticipation and aids in attaining easier sleep.

Alleviate Nightmares and Conquer Phobias

Each individual possesses a distinct fear or perhaps contends with the manifestation of unsettling nightmares. In certain instances, the presence of unsettling dreams pertaining to your apprehensions can disrupt your sleep patterns and result in restlessness. It is profoundly distressing, however lucid dreaming can serve as a mechanism of escapism and a coping tool. Lucid dreams provide an environment of security and tranquility, enabling individuals to effectively address distressing nightmares and conquer their apprehensions. One has the capability to exert control over their dreams through the practice of inducing lucid dreaming, thereby providing the means to ward off distressing nightmares. In the event that an individual experiences a state of heightened awareness within their dream, commonly known as a lucid nightmare, they possess the ability to alter the trajectory of the dream.

A considerable number of individuals employ lucid dreaming as a means to confront their fears. As the master of the dream realm, you possess the ability to deliberately evoke your fears within its confines, thereby providing yourself with a secure environment to confront and overcome them at your volition. As an illustration, let us consider the hypothetical scenario where one experiences arachnophobia, an intense aversion towards spiders. In this context, one can envisage the prospect of cautiously approaching a diminutive spider or encountering assorted arachnids. Subsequently, there is a possibility that you may have a dream wherein you find yourself grasping a spider, potentially progressing towards handling perilous arachnids. You have the ability to terminate the dream at any given moment and reestablish a state of security. Over time, you will discover that you are capable of calmly observing spiders in person without immediately fleeing the vicinity upon encountering one. Engaging in lucid dreaming expands the horizons of one's experiences, fostering a fearless approach to living.

A New Perspective

Lucid dreaming enables individuals to deliberate upon matters that they may otherwise disregard or relegate. During the state of lucid dreaming, individuals often engage in dialogues with their innermost self, where their mind and spirit interact and engage in profound introspection. They contemplate existential inquiries regarding the purpose that currently defines and will shape their future existence. Repressed thoughts have the potential to manifest during the state of lucid dreaming, affording individuals the chance to gain valuable insights and deepen their self-awareness. One gains a deeper understanding of oneself within an environment that provides security and the absence of scrutiny from others.

Dream Planning

In a lucid dream, one has the freedom to manifest any desired experience, and the added advantage lies in the premeditation of the dream's storyline prior to entering the state of sleep. Would you be interested in embarking on a submarine expedition to visit Atlantis? Certainly! How about embarking on a rappelling adventure at the majestic Grand Canyon or undertaking a heroic mission to thwart the nefarious plans of a super-villain and safeguard humanity? You are also capable of accomplishing that task.

Consider analyzing the narrative structure of your dream through the application of wake-induced or dream-induced techniques, which will be discussed in further detail at a later point. By employing these methods, you can adeptly fashion intricate dreams according to your personal inclinations. Expressing enthusiasm for a desired dream is prone to stimulating lucid dreaming, thus endeavor to generate a considerable degree of anticipation and regularly contemplate the dream you aspire to encounter.

Innovative Transportation Methods and Dimensions "

There is no imperative for you to engage in walking, driving, or employing any other commonly utilized modes of transportation within the realm of your lucid dreams. You have the freedom to choose your preferred mode of transportation! It is common for individuals to navigate through the expanses of their lucid dreams by means of solitary aviation or by whirling around and effortlessly arriving at their desired destinations. One has the opportunity to venture to foreign nations, fictional realms, unexplored temporal regions, or alternate planes of existence. Make an attempt to explore the occurrences of both the past and the future in your state of lucid dreaming, as you have the agency to operate within your preferred temporal framework without feeling obligated to adhere to any conventions of reality.

Meet Other People

Consider an individual whom you have long aspired to encounter. The identity of the person is immaterial, regardless of whether they are deceased or alive. One has the opportunity to encounter a range of individuals, both fictional and non-fictional, including superheroes, actors, activists, inventors, and other notable figures. The list is endless. You may direct your focus towards establishing new acquaintances and engage in strategic introspection prior to these interactions, thereby optimizing your cherished moments together. Consider the multitude of thought-provoking or scholarly discussions that one might engage in!

Encountering unfamiliar individuals within the realm of one's dreams is a truly remarkable experience; however, it is unnecessary to confine oneself to such encounters alone. A significant number of individuals encounter sexual imaginings within their conscious dreaming state, a revelation that astonishes them due to their steadfast commitment to exclusive intimacy with their respective significant other. This serves as a significant awakening for the majority of individuals due to their awareness of being in a dream state. Engaging in sexual fantasies may facilitate the induction of lucid dreaming, thereby serving as a viable strategy to pursue if one encounters difficulties in achieving lucidity during dreaming.